THE KORKU TRIBALS

CASTES AND TRIBES OF INDIA SERIES

No. 1. The Korku Tribals
by **S.G. Deogaonkar and Shailaja S. Deogaonkar**

No. 2. Socio-Cultural Study of Scheduled Tribes : The Pardhans of Maharashtra
by **S.R. Murkute**

CASTES AND TRIBES OF INDIA - 1

THE KORKU TRIBALS

S.G. DEOGAONKAR
S.S. DEOGAONKAR (Mrs.)

Foreword by
Prof. B.K. Roy Burman

CONCEPT PUBLISHING COMPANY, NEW DELHI-110059

ISBN 81-7022-297-4

First Published 1990

Shashishekhar Gopal **Deogaonkar** (*b*. 1938)
Shailaja Shashishekhar **Deogaonkar** (*b*. 1942)

Published by
Ashok Kumar Mittal
Concept Publishing Company
A/15-16, Commercial Block, Mohan Garden
NEW DELHI-110059 (India)

Lasertypeset by
Microtech Advance Printing Systems (Pvt.) Ltd.
H-13, Bali Nagar
NEW DELHI - 110015

Printed in India by
Taj Press
DELHI - 110006

FOREWORD

To me and many of my generation who had entered into the romance of anthropology through Calcutta University, Korku is not the name of just another tribe. To us the name triggers two processes : cognition of an empirical reality and affective gladiation back in time.

Our teacher, Prof. K.P. Chattopadhyay, who was one of the leaders of first generation of professional anthropologists of India, had visited the Korkus in Melghat forest in the 40's and produced a tract which gave us a glimpse of the holistic nature of anthropology. In this tract he linked up marriage on payment of bride-price that prevailed among the Korkus, with the emerging stratification system within the community. We felt proud of our teacher. But at the present time I have a depressing feeling that we do not feel anything for the Korkus. Those were the days when cultural relativism held the ground. The people were 'objects' of our research – not partners – in the continuous quest of humanity for luminating the meaning of man in the phenomenal world.

Even then Korku was something very special to our young minds, because of the association of the tribe with our teacher. In an anthropological exhibition which was held some time later, we depicted a Korku youngman, who was doing his love's labour, so that he could obtain his bride through service. The artist in our team had to grapple with the problem of representing both the ray of hope and the gloom of despair on his face.

Later in life, I visited the Korkus for a short while. It was a rush visit. I had no time to reflect; no time to delve into the deeper layer of my unremitted self. I, therefore, felt happy when Prof. Deogaonkar requested me to write the Foreword for their book on the Korkus. It had given me an opportunity to resume the journey in time; to go beyond the social mathematics of kinship, religion, economics, politics and so on.

Prof. Deogaonkar has provided a comprehensive descriptive account of the Korkus. We have the necessary facts to serve as the launching pad for anthropo-sociological imagination.

In the pre-British period, Melghat forest, the habitat of the Korkus, was a part of Nizam's State. In the distant past they seem to have been subjected by invaders, claiming to be Rajputs, who, however, did not occupy the land continuously. They collected tributes from the Korkus; and occasionally they led the Korkus in their raids on low-land villages from where they collected booty. Obviously, the relationship with the invaders was of the nature of confrontation and marginal accommodation.

The Korkus claim to be descendants of Ravana and call themselves *Ravanbansi*. On Diwali day they worship Ravana, Kumbhakarna and Meghnad. Now-a-days, however, they have included Rama in their pantheon. There is another figure, Bhimsen, looming in their supernatural terrain, as a tragic victim of the caprices of the High God, Mahadeva.

C.R. Prasad Rao and K.R. Murthy have in a recent publication – *Religious pluralism and social conflict : Social Change* (Vol. 18, No. 2, June 1988) highlighted two aspects of religious phenomenon in a pluralist context. These are : (a) its strictly theological or super-normal and transcendental elements and (b) its embodiment within the socio-economic and politico-historical context.

The second aspect seems to provide a clue to the understanding of the interesting features of Korku pantheon. As mentioned earlier, the Korkus have a historical relationship of confrontation and marginal accommodation with the invaders claiming to be Rajputs. If Rama was the source of legitimization of the right of the Rajputs to rule, Ravana was the symbol of resistance. But as the resistance weakened over time, Rama also got in, but without dislodging Ravana. If Ravana was the guardian angel of the Korkus, whose legendary history speaks of being oppressed by invaders from the North, in their cognitive world, there was another group of people, who were only oppressed but also suffered from social stigma. These were the people belonging to Mang caste. God created Bhimsen to save himself from embarrassment of accepting offerings from an untouchable Mang. Bhimsen was God's buffer against the untouchables and, also God's demoniac instrument to add to the misery of the Mangs. But this misery of the Mangs did not leave the Korkus unaffected. Bhimsen had to be accepted as an alter-ego of Ravana, under circumstances which do not project God in an eddifying manner. If Ravana was the anti-thesis of Rama, Bhimsen was the symbol of counter-culture against the unjust dispensation of the High God.

This leads to the theological aspect of Korku religion. The cognitive realm the Korkus recognize a High God. But as obvious from Korku mythology in the affective realm, the High God is not held very high. The vacuum in the affective realm is filled up by nature gods and incorporeal spirits, An Africa, scholar Mabuabu Duker has termed similar phenomenon in Africa as poly-monotheism, an existential humanistic culture (*Philosophy and social action*, Vol. 15, Nos. 1-2, 1989). One can trace features of the same in the rich lores of the Korkus, which were collected by Dr. (Mrs.) Deogaonkar and have been included in this book.

I have been benefited by going through the book and I hope many others who would read the book will feel the same way.

B.K. ROY BURMAN

PREFACE

The Korkus are a typical tribal population from the Amravati district of Maharashtra. They spread in the adjoining Betul and Nemad areas of Madhya Pradesh. This tribal group found only in the above parts, is in contrast with the other major tribal populations of the Vidarbha region of Maharashtra which consists mostly of the tribes of Dravidian ethnic origin like the Gonds, Pardhans, Kolams, etc. The Korkus are from the Munda group and as such display different characteristics. Due to historical and environmental reasons their level of acculturation is also high and their culture is strongly influenced by the culture of their Rajput chieftains.

It was an interesting experience to move through a mountainous area – the mythological abode of the Pandavas during *Agyatvas* in the Kingdom of King Virat. Worship of King Ravana of Lanka and his brother Kumbhakarna and brave son Meghnad is a typical feature of the Korku tribe. However, they also worship Lord Krishna, Hanuman and Shri Ram. The rich Korku folk-lore illustrates these phenomena.

We must mention that the study of the Korku tribals was instigated by Prof. R.K. Mutatkar, Professor of Anthropology, University of Poona, and we are grateful to him for his suggestion.

The Sr. Scientists of the Tribal Area Research Project of the P.K. Vidyapeeth, Akola, stationed at Dharni and Chikhaldara, gave full cooperation. We are particularly indebted to Dr. Varade, Dr. Malode, Mrs. Prema Kohad and Shri Hamid Khan for their co-operation. Shri V.K. Mohan, Divisional Forest Officer at Chikhaldara, and Shri Dharmadhikari, Principal, Forest Range Officers' Training College, Chikhaldara, were also extremely helpful in providing facilities and guidance.

As from the Korkus, Shri Arjun Jade Patel alias Arjun Guruji, a retired Korku teacher from Dahenda, and Shri Nandlal Patel Guruji from Dharni were extremely helpful in approaching villagers, interpreting songs, explaining situations and working as guides. 'Dalit Mitra' award winner Smt. Nanibai (Yashoda Mavaskar) of Dharni also gave useful help. Many other Korku men, women, boys and girls were enthusiastically helpful in collecting information. Shri L.D. Sonare of Toranwadi assisted in field-work.

We are extremely thankful to all these organizations, officers and individuals for their help and co-operation.

We are extremely thankful to Prof. (Dr.) B.K. Roy Burman for writing a 'Foreward' to this book.

Shri G.N. Roy, Principal, Aṇand Niketan College, Warora, and Shri S.G. Deshmukh, Librarian, deserve our sincere thanks for their help and encouragement. Shri M.S. Bodhe and Shri G.N. Dohade rendered the clerical-cum-typing assistance for which we are grateful to them.

With these words we place this book in the hands of our readers.

WARORA

(Dr.) S.G. DEOGAONKAR
(Dr.) Mrs. S.S. DEOGAONKAR

CONTENTS

LIST OF PHOTOGRAPHS

ONE

HABITAT OF THE KORKU TRIBALS

The Korku tribals are found only in Maharashtra and Madhya Pradesh, i.e., the central region in India. The Amravati district of Vidarbha region in Maharashtra lies between North 20° - 32° to 21° - 46° and East 76° - 38° to 78° - 27° and consists of Melghat, Amravati, Chandur Railway, Morshi, Achalpur and Daryapur tehsils. Melghat area is on the borders of Madhya Pradesh and spreads on the mountainous terrain of Satpura mountain ranges. It has two tribal blocks, viz., Chikhaldara and Dharni, and the Korkus are the chief inhabitants of these two blocks. In 1971 census their population was 67,742 and their concentration is only in the Melghat region of the Amravati district, their number in other districts of Vidarbha and Maharashtra is negligible.

The Korkus are a branch of the great Munda tribes and are placed here in the vicinity of other great tribe – the Gonds. Relatively they are at a better stage of acculturation and show a better socio-cultural level. The mountainous area, which is full of plateaus, mountains and valleys, reserved forest and many villages without approach roads, could not stagnate them.

A thorough anthropological study of this tribe covering all aspects of their social and cultural institutions including clan system, marriage and family, religious institutions, ceremonies and rituals, birth, death and funerary rights, etc., was undertaken. To complete the anthropological study, a study of the Korku dialect and literature, i.e., their folk-lore, has also been attempted.

Their Habitat and Population

The Korkus in Maharashtra are mainly concentrated in the Melghat area of Amravati district. They are supposed to be a spill over from the Korku tracts of Nemad and Betul districts from the Madhya Pradesh, though as a tribe it has identical origin and characteristics. However, their Melghat habitat has also a pretty long ethnological history belonging to bygone times.

The whole of the Dharni and Chikhaldara areas are on Gavilgad mountain ranges – a part of Satpura mountains – where there are small plateaus, and villages are situated either on plateaus or mountain slopes or valleys. The whole bus journey is through zig-zag roads, climbing up and down the heights varying between 1,000 to 3,000 feet (on an average) from sea level.

Melghat region in the Amravati district consists of a very high percentage of tribal population, the second largest area in the nine districts of Vidarbha, the first being the Gadchiroli district. Table 1.1 shows the position of total tribal and Korku population. (Tribe-wise break-up of 1981 Census is not available).

Table 1.1 : **Korku and other Tribal Population – As per Figures of 1971 Census**

	As per 1971	*As per 1981*
1. Total Scheduled Tribe population in Maharashtra	29,54,249	57,72,038
2. Total Korku population in Maharashtra	67,742	N A
3. Total Korku population in Amrawati district	67,713	N A
4. Percentage of total Tribal population in Melghat	79.37	N A
5. Percentage of Korkus in total population in Melghat	73.66	N A

Melghat area contains 345 villages out of which 146 are in Dharni and 199 in Chikhaldara.

In Melghat region the percentage and Tribal population as per 1981 Census figures is as under :

	Population	*Scheduled Tribe*	*Percentage of Tribal*
Total	1,42,810	1,06,277	74
Rural	1,40,190	1,05,686	74
Urban	2,620	591	22

Melghat Area : Geographical Description

The then Melghat tehsil, the northern tehsilof erstwhile Berar, was formerly part of the erstwhile Achalpur district, but since August 1905, incorporated in the Amravati district, lying between 20° 10′ and 21° 47′ N and 76° 38′ and 77° 40′ E, has an area of 4004.1 sq. km. (1,546 sq. miles). Prior to the transfer of Ambabarva State forest to the Buldhana district the area of the tehsil was 4224.2914 sq. km (1,631 sq. miles). The tehsil is also sometimes called Gangra and consists of that portion of the Satpura range situated between the Khamla plateau on the east and Jaitgad on the west with the rich valleys and low plateaus lying between the mountains. On the north it is bounded by Harsud and Bhaisdehi tehsils of Betul district and the Tapi river dividing it from Nimar district, on the south by the tehsils of Jalganv (Buldhana district), Akot (Akola district), Daryapur and Acalpur (of Amravati district), on the east again by Acalpur (Amravati district) and Bhaisdehi tehsil (of Betul district) and on the west by Burhanpur tehsil of Nimar district. Melghat tehsil is the richest in the forest reserves in the whole of the district. Fine quality timber is produced in the forests which has great demand outside and is chiefly exported to Bombay. Forest range offices have been established at suitable places and efforts to extend the forest area and grow quality timber trees are constantly made. The country is extremely rugged and broken into a succession of hills and valleys. In the more advanced portions, such as the neighbourhood of Dharni and Bairagad, where the rabi crops are grown, the green fields afford a pleasing and restful view to the eye. But the typical Melghat country consists of barren hills, scrub jungle and stony ground and is of a most dreary and desolate description. The villages are collections of hovels without any shade and one can well understand the feelings of the subordinate officials who regard the tract as *kalapani* and whose health requires frequent visits to the Berar plains. There are no navigable rivers in the tehsil except the Tapi which forms a portion of the boundary and may be considered such during the rainy season. The streams that drain the northern face of the range and fall into the Tapi river are the Sipna and the Kundu. Both have their rise close to the village of Khamla in Betul district, the former running south of Makhla plateau for 13 to 16 km (eight to 10 miles) takes a north-westerly course and passing through the villages of Harisal and Duni unites with the Tapi to the north-east of Amner; the latter passing through the Katkumb and Savligarh falls into the Tapi. The Garga rises under Vairat, and highest summit of the Gavilgad hills, and running nearly north-west throughout its course unites with the Tapi immediately under the southern face of the fort of Amner. The Kapra, the Majri and the Devan are the other minor streams which fall into the Tapi.

Climate

The climate of the tract has a very evil reputation, corresponding in this respect to the Dindori tehsil of Mandla and the Baihar tehsil of Balaghat. A severe type of malaria spreads at the end of the rainy season and the beginning of the cold weather. But with the successful implementation of the malaria eradication programme the conditions have considerably improved. In the hot weather the heat in the valleys is intense and the absence of shade, scarcity of water and the absence of shade, scarcity of water and absence of all the comforts of the plains make the tract most unpopular for touring purposes.

Population

The Melghat tehsil is the largest of all the tehsils of the district in size but the smallest of all in population. Its population in 1961 was only 72,779 while as per 1981 Census the total population was 1,42,810.

Soil and Agriculture

Regarding agriculture, soil area under different crops and the revenue system that existed then, the old Gazetteer of 1911 gives the following account :

> "In the valleys of the Tapi, Satpura and Gangra, especially in the neighbourhood of Dharni or Bairagad, rich stretches of black soil are to be found, and a visitor to either of these places, who sees spread out before him an unbroken expanse of wheat and gram, is liable to get a very misleading impression of the tract as a whole. The rest of the tract is of a very hilly and rugged description, though here and there pockets of black soil are seen in the valleys. The soils have never been thoroughly classified, but in 1897, Colonel Garrett's party classified a few typical fields in each village and worked out the average value of the soil for each village.

The soil as a whole is of the poorest description. Of the 338 villages three were valued at 12 annas per acre, 11 villages at 11 annas, 117 at values varying from six annas to nine annas, and the remaining 193 fell below six annas. In 1860-61, Mr. J. Mulheran in his statistical report on Gangra stated that rice and gram are the principal productions of Gangra and are grown expressly for export. The former is much prized by the people of Berar and Burhanpur, particularly the finest kind which resembles that grown in the Pilibhit district. Gram is exported principally to Burhanpur though large quantities are brought into Berar through all the passes by the people from Jalganv, Hivarkhed, Anjanganv, Acalpur and other places, south of the range. Jowar grows very luxuriantly near Kalambhar and other places in the Sipna and Garga valleys and also upon some of the lower plateaus. *Bardi, rala, margi, kodon kutki* and one or two other hill grains are grown upon more elevated slopes and plateaus and are used chiefly, if not entirely, by the Gonds. Potatoes are not cultivated by the Korkus of Gangra although that vegetable would pay them better than any other. What is sold at Chikhaldara and Acalpur is grown by the *Gavlis* residing at Chikhaldara, Sapur, Mota and Bori and by the Hindu inhabitants of the fort of Gavilgad. At this time the area under cultivation obtained by outlining and subsequent computation was 39,398.400 hectares (97,280 acres). In 1864, Captain Pearson referred to the rich soil and good cultivation of the plains near the Tapi and the Gangra, and the Gazetteer of 1870 states that 13 different kinds of grain were produced in the Melghat of which the most valuable were the finest wheat and rice, grown in large quantities. In 1906-07 the returns showed that out of a total of 6,72,667.280 hectares (16,63,376 acres) occupied for cultivation 57,645.270 hectares (142,334 acres) were under crop. Of this, cotton occupied 17,158.760 hectares (42,392 acres), jovar 5,618.345 hectares (23,749 acres) and wheat 3,342.870 hectares (8,254 acres). The area under rice was only 1,318.680 hectares (3,256 acres) and the total irrigated area was 20.23 hectares (50 acres). These figures do not include those for *inam*, leased and *jagir* villages, and are also not accurate measurement but are derived from the statistical calculation of 16 acres per plough."

Communication

The P.W.D. maintains road from Ghatang to Chikhaldara, the Gugumal forest road (Akot to Selu) and the Semadoh to Dharni road. These are first class roads with muram, partially bridged and drained. There are a good many roads maintained by the forest department. Perhaps the most important of these is the road running from Bairagad to Jhiri, 90.16 km (56 miles) in length. It is the principal line of export for the western portion of the Melghat, its claims for improvement deserve consideration. With a few exceptions every village in the Melghat is in cart communication with some main road; the tracts are rough and stony but they serve their purpose sufficiently well. The Khandva-Akola railway line passes through the south-western corner of the tehsil. Many new roads have been constructed under development schemes.

Chikhaldara

Chikhaldara, now a Tehsil and had Panchayat Samiti headquarters, is situated in latitude 21°29′ N and longitude 77° 22′ E and is a fine hill station in Amravati district. The plateau occupied by the civil station is about 1.2075 km (three quarters of a mile) broad and about 1.60 km (a mile) in length, but it has easy access to spacious table land surrounding it and to many picturesque valleys and there is ample scope for expansion. About 2.415 km (one and a half miles) to the south-west lies the trees of Gavilgad and Paratvada or Achalpur camp, the nearest town of any importance is reached by a variety of roads and footpaths, the best of which winds up through Ghatang and Silona with a fascinating scenery for a distance of 48.28 km (30 miles). Now buses ply on this route all the year round making travel more convenient and speedy. The rest-house at Ghatang was built in the days gone by to serve as a convenient half way halting place as only horse-carts or *tongas* could have access to the hill station. They, however, travelled at a very slow speed. The 34 kilometres (21 miles) surface road via Dhamanganv and Mota which marks the track followed by Wellesley's force in 1803 has since been converted into a thoroughfare. Chikhaldara is about 100 km (62 miles) distant from Amravati, the district headquarters, and is accessible by a fine motorable road.

Besides the fort, which commands several splendid views, Chikhaldara has little or no history. It has now been turned into a hill station and is the prominent summer health resort of the Vidarbha region. It was discovered, according to Nurul-Berar, by Captain Robinson of the Hyderabad Contingent Battery in A.D. 1823, the every year in which regular troops were first stationed at Achalpur, but bungalows were not built there till 1839. The height of the Chikhaldara hill station above sea level is 118.130 metres (3,666 feet). Its average mean maximum and minimum temperatures are 40.6°C (105°F.) and 1.7°C (35°F.), respectively. Even in the hottest month of the season a crisp and cool breeze almost always blows and except for a short period at noon, heat is never oppressive. The climate is pleasant during September and October. The average annual rainfall is 1905.60 mm (75"), almost all of which is received between June and September. Chikhaldara seems to have derived its present name from a valley to the east of Gavilgad fort, known as Kicklara. It is believed that Kichaka was killed here by Bhima during the Agyatvas (living incognito) of the Pandavas. It is often called as Chikhaldara also. The village variously known as Bairat or Vairat, lying 9.66 km (six miles) to the west of Chikhaldara is taken as synonymous with Viratanagari where Pandavas had so journed in disguise for one year during the period of their exile.

The popularity of the hill station was very soon established and Meadows Taylor mentions his delights as early as 1840 when he was there with the troops. He visited Acalpur again as the Deputy Commissioner on 9th December, 1857, and notes "how welcome were the large baskets of delicious peaches from Captain Hamilton's garden at Chikhalda and I wished I could go up there again and re-visit the old scenes". Peach is still cultivated in Amzari garden and the Company *Bagicha*, now popularly known as the Forest Garden, as it is under the management of the Forest Department, though it has degenerated considerably since Meadows Taylor's time. Coffee of the finest quality is grown in the public garden, formerly under the municipality but now taken over by the Forest Department, and in good many private gardens, especially on the land belonging to the Roman Catholic Mission. At one time a great future was anticipated from coffee and tea plantations at Chikhaldara. But the tea plantation has now entirely disappeared. Coffee plantation occupies an area of over 97,200 hectares (240 acres) and the Government is soon going to open a coffee plantation research centre. Besides peach cultivation, the Forest Garden contains various European and Tropical trees and shrubs, fruits and flowers. In a wild state roses, clematis, orchids, ferns and balsams, zinnias and ginger abound. On the upper plateau is situated the Chikhaldara Public Garden or Chikhaldara Bagicha covering an area of 5,260 hectares (13 acres). It is noted for very beautiful flowers and is the loveliest of the gardens at Chikhaldara. Good variety of mangoes, plums and peaches are grown in this garden. Among the trees the prominent are pine, cypress, silver-oak, eucalyptus, etc. At a distance of nearly 6.43 km (four miles) from Chikhaldara along the Chikhaldara-Paratvada road there is Amzari garden, supplying vegetables and fruits to the town of Chikhaldara. The principal difficulty in extending the plantation here is that of scarcity of water, though it has been considerably alleviated by pumping water into reservoirs from the Bir tank, which is the major source of water-supply.

Chikhaldara plateau is surrounded by many deep valley glades. The scenery is magnificent and the points of the station command, in turn, distant views of the Nimar and Mahadeva hills to the west and north and wooded valleys lying closer at hand to the Balaghat beyond. Foot-paths in the hillsides afford pleasant walks on the lower ridges, such as that to the Devil's Punch Bowl or Andhera Khord (the valley of Darkness), a splendid deep chasm walled in by a circle of cliffs 60 to 90 metres high, on one side of which, in the rains, tumbles a waterfall running up to the Bir tank. Close by is a fine triple-echo. Mountaineers exert themselves on many precipitous pathways and can even climb miniature Matheran, though one has to go more down than uphill to reach it. Three kilometres (two miles) away at the bottom of a secluded valley is Mariampur village.

Dharni

Dharni now a Tehsil and Panchayat Samiti Head-quarters was the largest village in the old Melghat tehsil with 628 houses and a population of 2,783 persons as per 1961 Census. It is the headquarters of Melghat tehsil and forms the terminus of the high road through the hills from Acalpur to Burhanpur. It is 96.540 km (60 miles) away from Acalpur and 148 km (92 miles) from Amravati. Dharni was noted for the malaria infested areas, but these have since been cleared of malaria and brought under cultivation. The land is very fertile, chief crops being wheat and gram. For irrigation, the river Tapi has been tapped here. Dharni tehsil is rich in timber forests and hence the State Government has established a timber depot here. Most of the timber after local consumption is chiefly exported to Bombay. There are offices of the tehsildar, State Electricity Board, Tribal Welfare Officer and the Panchayat Samiti. It has a branch of the District Co-operative Bank and two other Co-operative Societies. The village has a Primary

School, a multipurpose High School, a Post Office and a Police station. A dispensary is conducted by the *Zilla Parisad*, Recently a maternity home has been established.

Historical Account of the Administration of Melghat[1]

With the rest of Berar, Melghat came under British Administration in 1853 (from Nizam State). The population was almost entirely aboriginal, depending largely on '*dhaiya*', i.e., shifting cultivation.

In 1860-61, Mr. James Mutheran, in-charge of Topographical Survey Party, prepared maps for the whole tract. The whole tract was still under the revenue administration as per the Nizam Government.

In 1866, a Forest Department Division was organized on a report made by Captain Pearson and the Bairagarh forest (525 sq. miles) was demarcated, while in 1876 Gungurnal forest (300 sq. miles) was added. All Korkus and other aboriginals, who were then cultivating patches of land all over these forests, were induced to concentrate cultivation either inside the forests or in the remaining undemarcated area. All timber cutting operations were concentrated on this latter tract and the demarcated forests were subjected to strict protection. In 1877, Sir D. Brandis visited Melghat and advised that all idea of forest conservancy should be abandoned in the undemarcated forests, the only restriction suggested was that *dhaiya* cultivation should be prohibited, but grazing cultivation and extraction of timber and bamboos were subject to the payment of certain dues. Some rigid measures of conservancy were suggested in 1885-86 in closed forests and for fire protection but the effects on the Korku population were disastrous and prompt measures were necessary to see that the tract was not depopulated.

Up to 1888, a Sub-assistant Conservator held the appointment of Tehsildar. There was no distinction of forest and revenue villages. Mr. W.B. Jones, Commissioner, said in 1879 : "It is *raiyatwari* system with many of the evils of other systems and a few of its own disadvantages. The Government, though nominally dealing with the *raiyats*, really leaves them unprotected and exacts its revenue from *patels* through alien *patwaris*, asking no further questions. The *patel* is thus a *malguzar* with name of the advantages of his position : the cultivator-tenant of the State with few of the advantages of that position.[2] The *patwaris* were practically Tehsildars in their circles.[3]

Between 1883 - 86, Melghat was surveyed by the Imperial Forests Survey Department. Land Records in Berar submitted proposals for a regular settlement of the greater part of Melghat and for preparation of the usual village registers.

The fugitive nature of the Korku cultivation and the risk of disturbing those aboriginals ever put forth as obstacles in the way of settlement and it was not realized that cultivation was stable in certain parts of Melghat, and that the existing system left the aboriginals without any protection against the usurper and land grabber who were gradually ousting them from all the best land.[4]

On 29th March, 1909, the Chief Commissioner issued orders dealing with all important questions. Deputy Commissioner and Sub-Divisional Officers were to allot lands to the residents of Melghat village or neighbouring village, preference being given to aboriginals and no land was to be allotted except to bona fide agriculturist, among whom members of following classes shall not be reckoned; viz., Marwaris, Barrias, Kalars, Brahmins. Working plan for the Melghat Division was completed in 1914-15 and Mr. C.V. Wills, I.C.S., was deputed to examine it and make recommendation. These were passed in 1916. Revision settlement operations followed in 1925.

Aboriginal tribes/Backward classes in Melghat *taluq* as in 1911 were :[5]

(1) Korku	(2) Balai
(3) Mahar	(4) Gond
(5) Bhil	(6) Gaolan
(7) Nihal	(8) Gaoli
(9) Banjari	(10) Pardhan
(11) Moghia	(12) Gosai
(13) Gowari	(14) Korku Christians
(15) Chamar	(16) Bhut
	(17) Mang.

An occupant shall be allowed to take Mahua free from any part of the village area. An aboriginal occupant may cut and dispose of any tree in the land occupied by him save the following trees on nala banli : Mango, Mahua, Achar, Jamun, Harra, Kusam, and the fruit bearing tendu.

The Sub-Divisional Officer would appoint a *patel* for every village with a non-hereditary tenure with due regard to local customs, an aboriginal *patel* for a predominantly aboriginal population and vice versa.

REFERENCES

1. Melghat Manual, 1929. A Government. of India Publication for office use during the British Regime, p. 1.
2. *Ibid.*, p. 2.
3. *Ibid.*, p. 3.
4. *Ibid.*, p. 4.
5. *Ibid.*, p. 5.

TWO

PHYSICAL ENVIRONMENT AND MATERIAL CULTURE

Physical Features and Appearance

The Korkus are of medium height, slightly taller than Gonds, well-built and muscular. On an average they have a round face, a wide nose but not much flat.

Anthropometric Indices of Korkus[1]

		mm
(1)	Head (Circumference)	526-57
	Ratio/Cephalic index	77 : 38
(2)	Nose/Height	108.95
	Ratio of length and width of nose	89 : 24
(3)	Length of upper jaw	47.37
(4)	Ratio of the width of face and head	84 : 12

Korkus have a dark complexion.

Dress

Traditionally the Korkus put-on a loin cloth and a wisp of turban coiled on the top of the head in which they used to put a brass chain. Keeping thé head uncovered is considered a bad sign and hence they put some cloth – even torn – on the head. Rarely the men use shirts or coats and these days mostly use *dhotis*. The women use white or bright coloured *lugda* and take one end on the breast but may not use *choli* (or blouse).

The modernized Korku boys and girls usually put on the common urban dress like *pyjama* and shirt or pant, manila, coat, etc. The girls also wear five-yard *saris*, blouse, etc. Cotton clothes are common. Children put on a half-pant (*chaddi*).

Ornaments

They are loaded with ornaments made of brass, iron, alloys and, in case of rich Korkus, even silver. Beeds of glass and stones are woven into *mala* and their necks are full of such necklaces and *malas*. Woman from *Patels* 'and Police-*patels*' houses were using silver ornaments also.

Sutra, Payari, Bichhia, Mudi, Kada, Nigdi, Pairpatti (Painjan) Machhi are very popular ornaments. In nose they put a *Besar* made of brass, ear-rings (*Karnaful*) in ear made of German-silver, at least 16 bangles and a bracelet of German-silver, and finger-rings, etc., are common. A chain joins the nasal ring to the earing or goes to the hair on the head. In the foot they put on a brass ring (*Kada*). Previously eight to ten brass rings were put around the ankles but it is now rare.

Even the men used to wear a large brass ring in one ear (*Bali*).

Women invariably wear all ornaments during important festivals.

Tatooing

Men don't get tatooed but the women have tatooing on hand, i.e., on the forearm and they have designs of different flowers, trees, peacock, or triangles, rectangles or other animals; and three spots (points) on the fore-head. It is considered as a sign of *Saubhagya* (a good omen for a married woman for a long life to her husband). They believe that the gates of heaven will not be lifted for a woman who has no tatooing.

The Korku women don't apply *Kumkum*; though now they are adopting it.

Huts

Their villages are neat and clean and spread along sides of one long street. On an average there are 20 huts. The average hut is about 15-20 sq. feet and is built of bamboo or wooden walls with mud or cow-dung paste spread over the walls. Roofs are flat, covered with loose grass over a layer of leaves and pressed by poles. These days indigenous tiles are also used. The walls for some wealthy folks' huts may be of bricks. But an average Korku lives in a thatched hut which does not offer much protection during rainy season. It was found during fieldwork that most of the houses were thatched with grass or tiles and only *Patels* or rich Korkus had used bricks for their houses.

Utensils

Hollow bamboos, dried gourds are used but earthenware utensils are common for storage and cooking. They use brass utensils and german-silver (i.e., aluminium) utensils. All the respondents from Dharni as well as Chikhaldara blocks reported that they were using earthenwares, aluminium (which they usually call German' – a mini form of the term german-silver) and brass utensils; in addition to dried leaves gourds, etc.

Occupation

It is believed that many years ago the Korkus were nomads but since the known history they are settled. They still practise hunting but have stopped shifting cultivation. Some of them are land-owners and cultivators but others work as labourers on farms.

Usually they are not cattle keepers and very few keep buffaloes or cows. Only bullocks are kept for agriculture. By nature they are improvident and lazy. They grow only lighter grains in the hilly tracts and on slopes but are not agriculturists in real sense. They grow *Juar, Kutki, Barbati, Toor*, etc. Wheat is rarely grown where soil is black, but mostly the soil is red with stones in lower layer.

The Korkus in Dharni block are comparatively well-off and have progressed well. The soil in some parts of the Dharni block is black and they can get two crops. A few Korkus reported cotton crop where there is black-soil but this is hardly five per cent. The Chikhaldara tribals are comparatively poor and are not economically in a good condition.

Food Habits

As his morning meal, an average Korku eats *juar* soup prepared by boiling *juar* flour in water. Only salt is put in it. This is called *Ghato* or *Pejo* by them. Mahua flowers are fried or roasted and eaten along with *Pejo*. Their evening meal consists of a bread made of *juar* or *kutki* flour, some wild leafy vegetables and chillies may also be used. They purchase edible oil and wheat as per their needs and as the purse permits. Fowls, pork, fish, crabs, buffalo, pig, birds are eaten.

Handicrafts

No special handicrafts or secondary occupations are reported. Laziness can be one of the reasons.

They prepare their own traditional agricultural implements and thus know limited carpentry and smithy.

Some carvings on the Mundas erected at Sidoli with images of forefathers or other animal figures, etc., are witnessed. Their skill in handicrafts may be considered as limited to these things only.

Characteristic Habits

The Korkus are honest but not hard-working. They are easily cheated. Drunkenness is very common. The Dharni Korkus are in a better economic condition due to good black soil. They get good crops. When needed they borrow from money-lenders. Even then they are not progressing well.

The reason is the exorbitant borrowing rates. If hundred rupees are borrowed for three to four months, they have to return Rs. 150 to 200 after four months. Similarly they are drunkards and waste money on wine. Hence, their economic condition does not improve.

Those who are agricultural labourers can also lead a good life. But they pledge the ornaments, borrow and spend on drinking. Day-by-day their economic condition is thus deteriorating.

When rains are uncertain many Korkus even don't get wages and then it is difficult for them even to sustain family.

Sacrifices are very common even for minor worships and on large-scale during ceremonies and festivals. The animals mostly sacrificed are chickens, goats, fowls, etc.

During study it was reported that they like eating rabbits, goats and pigs (particularly wild-pigs) and deer which is costly these days due to stringent forest laws.

When asked whether eating some animals is taboo, they reported cows, buffaloes, jackals and bears as such. They consider the *Goyaras* as outcastes because they eat beaf. However, they sacrifice a buffalo on the Dussehra day and eat its flesh. On the whole, the taboos are not very strict but just conventions.

Water

Drinking water is not easily available to all villages in all areas. Mostly there are *nullahs* or rivulets or rivers and people fetch water from these natural sources. In some villages, wells are available and at many places tube-wells are dug which supply drinking water to all villagers. Rest of the villages have other sources of water. Technology has thus reached the villages.

Trees

Most of the villages are situated in or in the vicinity of reserved forest. In every village there are many trees either in the farms or premises of Korkus, or in the adjacent forest. Most popular and common trees are : Mahua, Tendu, Teak; next come Shravan, Dhavda, Mango, Neem and Jagni, etc. Some of their septs are based on trees.

REFERENCE

1. Karve, Irawati (Dr.) (1962). *Marathi Lokanchi Sanskriti*, Deshmukh & Co., Pune, (2nd Ed.), p. 130.

THREE

THE ETHNOLOGICAL ANTECEDENTS OF THE KORKU

Their Ethnic Roots

The Korkus (also spelt as Kurkus) belong to the Munda family and are considered the most 'westward Munda-speaking tribes', and are widely separated from the main block of linguistically related tribes. Actually they are very near to the Gond and related tribes of Vidarbha and Madhya Pradesh. They are of Austric origin and R. Mukherjee calls them either of Austric or of Nigroto language group. He has also found Proto-Austroloid characteristics in them like flat nose, curly hair, thick lips and black complexion.

Russel and Hiralal consider Korkus as a Munda or Kolarian tribe akin to the Korwas, with whom they have been identified in Indian Census of 1901[1] The language of Korwas which is another Munda tribe in Chota Nagpur is also known as Korku or Kurku and one of their sub-castes has the same name.[2] Some Korakus or Movasis are found in Chota Nagpur (habitat of Hill Korwas) and Colonel Dalton considered them a branch of Korwas, Sept names of Korkus are in many cases identical with those of the Kols and Korwas and hence it is also believed that Korkus and Korwas are the same tribe and both of them may be off-shoots of the great Kol or Munda tribe.[3] Migrating much further than their kinsmen, long past, they must have come to the West on the Mahadeo or Satpura hills. Hence there lies a large expanse between them and the Kols and Korwas, which is occupied by the Gonds and other tribes with considerable sprinkling of Kols in Mandla, Jubalpur and Bilaspur.[4]

W.H.P. Driver, who listed 13 *gotras* or septs among Korkus, also points out that they are closely related to Korwas.[5]

G.A. Grierson in volume IV "Munda and Dravidian Languages" of his *Linguistic Survey of India* lists 14 dialects under the Munda family and includes Korwa and Korku dialects under the group.[6] He also calls both these dialects as being from the Santhali tradition once known as Kherwarian languages the only difference being the dis-use of 'h' in Korku and allied dialects.[7] Thus, they are considered akin to the Kols of Chota Nagpur and the Santhals of Santhal parganas.[8]

On the above background, one is baffled when efforts are made to equate them with Gonds who are of Dravidian origin. However, it is interesting to note that long back the Sanskrit scholar, Max Muller, wrote: "I can see many coincidences between Uraon, Rajmahali and Gondi on the one side and Sinhabhum, Sontal, Bhumji and Mundala words on the other . . . . Both are two different races . . . which came in contact in these regions . . . with ethnic name 'Munda'." Hodgson classified the languages under the head 'Tamulian'. Ho, Santali, Bhumji, Kurukh and Mundari are considered as dialects of Kol languages. Logan also followed Hodgson and called them as North Dravidian.[9] Grierson mentions that some anthropologists consider Munda and Dravidas as of the same race. He also states that the principal home of Munda languages at present is Chota Nagpur plateau and speakers are also found in adjoining districts of Madras, Central Province (now M.P.) and Mahadeo Hills (i.e., Satpura ranges). This explains the reason behind the classification of Korkus or Korwas as being of Dravidian origin.

Meaning of 'Korku'

'Koru' means man and 'Ku' is a plural termination, thus Korku means the tribes men.

According to another interpretation 'Koro' means road, and 'Ku' means a man, that is, a street-man or a wanderer. This meaning hints to the historical fact that while wandering away from their kinsmen they came to this area.

Korkus also claim their origin to the Kurus or Kauravas of the *Mahabharata* period (or Korwas ... ?), thus trying to link their origin to Aryan race. Some also link them to the 'Kaurava' kings of *Mahabharata* period.

The Korkus of Nemad (M.P.) trace their origin to the great mythological snake 'Karkotaka' and also worship snake, hinting at their origin in the Naga race.

Some Melghat Korkus consider themselves as '*Ravanavanshi*', i.e., having their ethnic origin from King Ravana.

Some consider their origin from the Chauhan clan of Rajputs. They also say that they ran away from the battle-field and were chased by Muhammedans. When asked as to who were they, one of them just uttered 'Korku'. Believing that they were nót Rajputs they were allowed to be free.

They used to move like nomads in early years but later settled down.

THEIR SOCIAL ORGANIZATION

The Korkus are considered to be divided into four sub-divisions or sub-tribes, mainly on territorial basis, but akin to caste distinction. These are Bawaria, Ruma, Bondoya and Muasi or Movasi. Russel and Hiralal consider Movasi as the largest sub-division of the Korkus which means a 'troubled country' and meant 'a robber' to Marathi ears as they used to attack and rob people living in the low plains of Berar. Hislop states that the name Movasi came from mahua tree.

Raj Korku has also been stated as a land-owning caste, the remaining called Potharia. Out of the four sub-divisions, the Bawarias were mostly concentrated in Betul, the Ruma in the Amravati district and Bondoyas in Jitgarh and Pachmarhi tract. Some believe that Movasi and Bawaria are high castes and are collectively known as Raj Korkus.

Another version is of four major septs or groups, viz., Ruma, Potadya, Dularya and Khoberi or Bobai. Within Ruma Korkus there are again sub-types, viz., Kora (man), Saraku, (monkey), Bana (Bear) and Ruma. Rumas consider themselves the descendants of Mundari origin.

Sub-septs and Clan

The four sub-septs found in the Melghat area are: *Ruma, Bondoya Movasi* and the *Goyara*. As the report goes, long ago Korkus had only three sub-septs, viz. Movasi, Rumba/Ruma and Bondoya. They used to kill buffaloes during Dussehra festival and eat buffalo flesh but did not eat beaf (cow-flesh). Later, some Korkus started eating beaf and thence-forth such Korkus were called '*Goyara*'. The other three shunned all relationships with the *Goyara* and treated them as down-castes. Thus, four septs or phrateries came into existence, viz., Ruma/Rumba, Movasi, Bondoya and *Goyara*. Thus, in Melghat the sept *Goyara* is reported as an inferior sub-sept of the Korku.

The Myth of Creation of Social Order

There is a myth about the creation of clans (*Gotras*) among the Korkus. The Korkus lived like brothers and sisters for many years. Tired of that life, and being aroused with sex-drive they went to Lord Shiva and asked him how could they be happy. Lord Shiva yawned and a strange thing happened. He took the form of a ferocious lion. Frightened by this form, all of them ran hither-thither for shelter and everyone tried to hide behind whatever could be found in the jungle. After the things calmed down, Lord Shiva again appeared in usual form and all Korkus came out of their hide-outs. They gathered around, Lord Shiva then he told them that the object which was used as shelter by each one shall be his *Gotra* (clan). Thus particular trees, grass, soil, stone and other animate or inanimate objects, etc., became the names of their clans. He also ordained them to marry outside the clan, thus making the clans exogamous. This story is narrated by some other authors in a slightly different form – the variation being in the reasons for running helter-skelter and hiding.

Another interpretation hints of a great battle in which their ancestors were defeated and took refuge behind trees and other articles.

The Clans

It is believed that originally these were totemic septs but later were connected by Korkus to their ancestors through the above legend. The reported number of these clans varies as per different authors. Russel and Hiralal report that each sub-caste consists of 36 septs.[10] Driver and John Drake report 121/2 clans but also add that the actual clan names excede this figure. John Drake also opines that this quoted figure of 121/2 clans may be due to Gond influence, which seems plausible as in Gonds they have 12 clans.[11]

In the present study Sixteen totemic clans (Gotras) were discovered which are as shown in Table 3.1.

Shri Arjun Jade Patel, who is a *Bhumka* and an old retired teacher also confirmed that there are only sixteen 'Gotras'.

It is reported that *Bethe, Kasda, Movasi, Dhi, Jambu, Mara* and *Sakom* are very common. *Kasada* and *Movasi* gotras are considered as auspicious and naturally get priority in social and religious ceremonies. *Tota* is considered as inauspicious.

Table 3.1: **Korku Totemic Clans (Gotras)**

	Clan (Gotra)	*Meaning of the term*
1.	Bethe	Biba/Bhilawa tree
2.	Jambhu	Jamun tree (*Eugenia jambolana*)
3.	Bhusum	Grass
4.	Kasda/Kasa	Soil/earth
5.	Mauvasi	Water
6.	Dhikar	Tree
7.	Selu	Tree
8.	Chilati	A Creeper (*Caesalpinia sepiaria*)
9.	Korilua	A Tree
10.	Sakom	Leaf
11.	Tota	Maize
12.	Chuthur	Honey
13.	Takher	Cucumber
14.	Koliya	Coal
15.	Chathwa	Athoa/Athole (a wooden ladle)
16.	Mara	Peacock/Peafowl.

Gotras found in the same area, e.g., *Jambhu* (Jamun tree) and *Dhi* tree are found on the river banks, i.e., together in the same area and hence were considered as brother-gotras (Phrateries ?) and hence marriages between them were not possible. However, now these restrictions are rare and only marriages within the same gotra is tabooed.

It is interesting to note that 'Thakur' has been reported as a gotra by some investigators which in fact is a Rajput sub-caste found in Uttar Pradesh and Rajasthan. This could only result from adoption through introjection. This supports the statement of Russel and Hiralal which states that the bands of Korkus often led by the Rajput chieftains, and settling on the high hills, collected payments from the low land villages of Berar, which was known as '*Tankha Movasi*'. 'Movasi' means the troubled country. The Movasi among Korkus claim the highest rank and formerly practised armed robbery.[12]

John Drake is probably nearer to Russel and Hiralal when he states that the Korkus occasionally seek to establish a Rajput ancestory. Analysing the truth behind this claim he further says that 'the element of truth seems to be that some measure of intercourse has taken place, resulting in the loss of caste on the part of individual Rajputs and their identification with the Kurku people'.[13] The Raj Korku sept regarded with honour – and as Russel and Hiralal report, even Brahmins accept water from them – contains wealthier and more powerful members of the tribe, and is likely to be a product and of Rajput-Korku relationship.[14]

The ethnic relationship between the Korwas and Korkus outlined earlier also supports this theory. The Hill-Korwas have a historical myth about their clan origin which states that seven Baghel Kshatriya brothers who first entered the Khuria region as hunters settled there as rulers of Hill Korwas, and later, on being threated by the natives, gave up their identity, married Korwa women and from that time the present five-clan set-up of Hill Korwas came into being.

The various septs and different numbers given above are from various parts of the region of Korku habitat, viz., Nemad (Nimar), Hoshangabad and Betul districts of Madhya Pradesh and Melghat region of the Amravati district of Maharashtra. Stephen Fuchs, who visited the Korkus of Melghat in 1939 and thereafter, had reported 13 clan names among the Korkus of Melghat – particularly in villages around Chikhaldara (Chikhalda – as it was then pronounced). Out of these thirteen, seven referred to bushes, trees or their products, four to inanimate objects, one meant a pass between two hills and the meaning of one was not known.[15]

The present study was conducted in villages around Chikhaldara and Dharni, i.e., two blocks – and as such the finding of 16 septs or clans sounds reasonable as well as plausible on the background of the above discussion. The variations in the number of septs reported is either due to repetitions (e.g., *Rumba* or *Movasi* are also reported as septs) or due to contaminated reporting, mistakes in pronunciation, joining of pre-fixes or suffixes by fancy of reporters, etc. The experts in Korku social history and mythology from the area, however, support only *sixteen* septs.

The sub-sept or sub-caste *Goyara* has not been reported earlier in any work on Korkus and seems to have originated in later years. As observed by Mr. Crosthwaite, in Hoshangabad area, four-fifths of the Korkus were so affected 'by the spread of Brahminical influence as to have ceased to differ in any marked way from the Hindu element . . . as to be ashamed of calling themselves Korkus.[16] Ferriera also maintains that although their beliefs and practices are evidently of a different origin, they regard themselves as Hindus.[17] May be this strong cultural identification with the Hindu concepts was responsible for the condemnation of the *Goyaras* and treating them as almost out-castes.

Out of the sub-tribes *Ruma* or *Rumba* account for the maximum number in the area, followed by *Movasi* and *Bondoya*. Similarly *Kasda, Bethe, Dhi, Jambhu* and *Chilati* are the more common septs.

TOTEM AND TOTEMISM

As seen earlier the septs or clans among Korkus are based on animate or inanimate objects and hence these clan-names sound totemic. However, no other evidence of totemism is found among them. No totem taboos or distinctly totemic usages other than these clan names were found.[18]

Similarly, in the present study hardly any one reported any totemic usages connected with individual or group life.

Association of totemic ideas in the tatoo designs, drawings on door or roof or any other conscious use or worship of any such object was distinctly absent, and, when asked, all gave a negative reply.

REFERENCES

1. Russel and Hiralal, (1975). *Tribes and Castes of the Central Provinces of India*, III, Cosmo Publications, Delhi, Reprint, p. 550.
2. *Ibid*.
3. *Ibid*., p. 551.
4. *Ibid*.
5. Ferriera, J.V., (1965). *Totemism in India*, Oxford University Press, Bombay; p. 115.
6. Grierson, G.A., (1967). *Linguistic Survey of India*, IV, Motilal Banarsidas, First Reprint, p. 169.
7. *Ibid*.
8. Drake, John, (1914). 'Kurkus' in *Encyclopaedia of Religion and Ethics*, VII, James Hastings (Ed.), T & T Clark, New York, p. 720.
9. Grierson, G.A., *op.cit*.
10. Russel & Hiralal, *op. cit*., p. 554.
11. Drake, John, *op. cit*., p. 760.
12. Russel & Hiralal *op.cit*., p. 551.
13. Drake, John, *op.cit*.
14. Russel & Hiralal, *op.cit*., pp. 551-52.
15. Ferriera, J.V., *op. cit*.
16. Russel & Hiralal, *op. cit*., p. 655.
17. Ferriera, J.V., *op. cit*., p. 116.
18. *Ibid*., p. 115.

FOUR

LIFE-CYCLE RITUALS

Birth

The birth of child takes place in their homes. One old lady called *Sayani-budhi* (a wise old lady) helps by massage. In one corner of the house a ditch is dug in which the water after the bath of the mother and child is collected. This is for the first five days. On the fifth day the *Sayani-budhi* worships the *Chatti*-God and turmeric, *kumkum*, biba, seasamum, tin and coconut are offered to the God and after the *puja* all are put in the ditch which is then filled up and closed. Then the head of the family names the child. Name giving is done on the fifth day.

It is also reported that during the first five days of child birth the father is barred from entering the house and compelled to rest in the shelter of cuttle-shed or such place which, normally, is not used for habitation.

On the fifth day (*Panchvi*), *Panchas* are invited and a round pot full of water (*Kalash*) is kept in front of the child. All pray and bow before the *Kalash*. *Panchas* put coins in it. A dinner is given to all.

On the 12th day the mother, along-with the child, is taken to a river bank where child and the mother are bathed and return home, after which the mother resumes her normal routine.

Rebirth

Korkus believe in rebirth. Almost 90 per cent respondents reported that before burial a few drops of oil are dropped on the dead body or charcoal is used to make markings on the body or face of the dead body. Later, if these marks are seen on the new born child it is believed that the person has reborn.

Marriage

Marriages are normally settled by either of the two types viz., (1)

Match marriage – settled by parents or (2) Catch marriage – in which the boy and girl make their own choice, the usual meeting place being Bazar (*Hati*).

In the first type, the parents of the boy have to search for a suitable girl. This is called *Bali Dhundna* (girl searching). After finding a suitable girl they enquire about her and her family and consult the Patel and other elders from the village. Marriages being exogamous they also enquire about the *Gotra* to decide whether the marriage is possible between their septs. After this, a formal approach is made to the parents of the girl which is called *Mangni* (*Mangna* in Hindi means to demand). For this purpose a *Panchayat* is called which consists of the parents of the boy, girls' parents and other elderly persons from the girls' village including the Patel of that village. The intermediary who is called *Chitulya* or *Chithodya* is important in these negotiations.

Bride-price

On a fixed day the *Panchayat* meets and settles the marriage. The *panchas* collect some rupees (normally Rs. 25) from the boy's father which is spent for serving *Gud* (Jaggery) and/or liquor to *panchas* and this is called *Gudpan*. In this very meeting *Gonom* (bride-price) is also settled. This includes cash (about Rs. 1,000 to Rs. 1,200 or so), foodgrains and a good bullock which is called a '*Mundo*'. The boy's party has to agree to make all these payments. Then engagement is fixed.

After four to six months from engagement the actual marriage ceremony follows. The function is performed at the boy's place and full expenses are borne by him.

The girl's party goes to the boy's village. However, there is another custom according to which the boy's party goes to the girl's place where the marriage is performed. In some cases the boy and the girl run away and start living together and the actual marriage may be performed at leisure.

The Ritual

A special *Mandap* (*Pandal*) is erected at boy's place which has twelve wooden pillars (stumps) out of which one is of *Salai* (*Bosvellia serrata*), one of *Moha* and one of *Gullar* trees. The rest nine stumps may be of teak or other lesser quality trees. On the roof of the *pandal* are spread the branches and leaves of *Jamun* tree. At girl's place also a *pandal* on nine-stumps is erected.

Bhumka – their traditional priest – performs the marriage. As the Korkus consider Monday and Friday as auspicious days they perform marriages preferably on these two days. These days, Sunday or Thursday, are also selected as per convenience.

Most of the marriages are performed in the Hindu calendar months of *Chaitra* and *Vaisakh* (March to May). However, they avoid marriages during Bhavai festival which falls in *Vaisakh*, as that is considered as inauspicious.

In the second type of marriage the boy meets the girl in bazar or some other place and makes his own selection with her consent. There are no youth dormitaries or similar institution. The bazar before Diwali which is called *Bhongdu-Hati* is more popular for this purpose. If they select each other the boy elopes with her and takes her to his house and they start living as husband and wife. On learning about this the girl's parents go to boy's place with *Panchas* and demand *Gonom* (bride-price) which may reach up to Rs. 1,500. On payment, the marriage is accepted by all and no formal marriage ceremony is essential.

A typical custom in Korkus as reported is that before the boy's party starts for the girl's village, a blanket is spread in the courtyard of the house and the bride-groom and his elder brother's wife are made to stand on it and embrace each other seven times. This ceremony is considered by Russel and Hiralal as survival of the modified system of polyandry, under which the younger brothers are allowed access to the elder brother's wife until their own marriage. This ceremony thus should typify the cessation of intercourse between them at the wedding of the boy.

The *wedded* couple is covered with a blanket and water is poured upon them. The boy ties a necklace around the girl's neck and the couple is lifted and taken three times around the yard of the house. This much should normally be the tribal custom. However, due to adoption of practices from the neighbouring areas, rice-throwing and taking seven steps (*Saptapadi*) have also entered their rituals. Bathing and applying turmeric powder are important in marriage. The bridegroom lifts the bride and dances. All men and women also dance and women sing *Airan* song which is full of vulgar abuses. Men play on flute and *Dhol*.

Child marriages are not observed but a girl is married between the age of 12 to 18 years. Polygamy is in vogue but is now getting obsolete.

Widow Remarriage and Divorce

Widow remarriage is allowed and divorce is simple but a *Panchayat* is to be called for deciding on divorce.

When a man marries a widow he has to pay half the usual bride-price, i.e., Rs. 500-750 to her or to her parents, and then he can bring her to his home.

For divorcing a wife a *Panchayat* is called and it imposes a fine of Rs. 25 on the man who wants to divorce his wife after which the divorce is approved.

Lamanya or Lamjanya

This is an institution connected with bride-price. If a boy is not in a position to pay bride-price he has to serve for a fixed period which may range from one to two years and thus render services in lieu of money and he is called *Lamjanya*. This is settled before *Panchas* from both sides. When a boy runs away with the girl, the girl's parents reach his place and demand bride-price which may range between Rs. 1,000 to Rs. 1,500. If the boy or his father is not in a position to make the payment, the boy has to go as *Lamjanya*. He may borrow from a *Sahukar* (money-lender) and serve at his place to make good repayment of the amount.

The Family

Cellular families are not uncommon. A married son may live separately. Though women are well-treated there is patriarchal system and children get the sept and clan name of the father.

Inheritance is to the widow and the unmarried sons and the daughters have no share in the property.

Though polygamy is traditionally practised it is very rare that cases of polygamy (that too only two wives) are found.

Number of children per couple varies between three to seven, average being of five children.

Death and Funerary Rites

The Korkus bury the dead. This is in consonance with their myth of creation of mankind in which the crow *Kagbhusundi* or *Kagliamasa* had promised to return the borrowed earth. '*Dust thou art, and thy dust returnest*' is possible with burial. Though there are burial grounds where the ordinary people are buried, some persons from the family are buried in their own field along with their dear things. Some people cremate the dead bodies which is more common among the modern-ized.

Three slightly different versions are reported regarding the funerary rituals. Let us know them one by one.

The dead body is bathed and a new *dhoti* cloth is rapped around it and a *pal* of two logs or bamboos is prepared on which the dead body is tied. All the members from the family of the deceased offer some food, water and coins/money to the body and bow down. Then four *pal*-bearers carry the body to the burial place where a ditch of man's size is dug and body is interred to rest in peace. The ditch is then filled-up with stones, earth, pounding it firmly. Some branches of thorny shrubs and trees are kept over it – to keep animals away. Some food, *khichdi* and water is also kept there. While returning, all mour-ners go to some nullah, river or well and take bath. Then the head of the family contributes Rs. 15 and Rs. 2 are contributed by other families and liquor is bought from that contribution and all drink it. Then all of them return to the house of the deceased and every one throws some water on fire over his head and returns after consoling the family members of the deceased's family. On the third day meals and water are kept near the burial place for the dead person.

Sidoli/Phool-Jagni

Within four to five years from the death a function called *Sidoli* is per-formed which is meant to give satisfaction to the departed soul. A three feet long and about six inches thick log of teak wood is brought and an image of the deceased is carved on it. This is called '*Munda*' which is brought home and a goat is sacrificed before it. The house is cleaned and brightened and on the next day all men and women take that *Munda* on shoulders and dance, using abuses and vulger words for each other. The songs are sung which also contain abuses. People from other villages also come for dancing. All of them go out of the village while dancing where all assemble and a goat is brought and tied to a pole at the centre. The Patel of that town then wields an axe and severs off the head of the goat in one stroke from body. The persons from neighbouring villages get four kilo flour of *juar* and people from the village are served with *juar* bread and mutton. On the next day the *Munda* is carried to some place outside the village and buried straight. Thus the *Sidoli* is celebrated. It is celebrated for a dead *Bhumka*, or married rich men.

According to another version, they either cremate but mostly bury the dead. On returning from burial ground they prepare an idol of flour and offer turmeric powder, wine and rice to the idol. Neighbours and relatives join in this offering. If some elderly person from the house has passed away the function called '*Phool-Jagni*' is performed which may be even after one or two years from death, normally in a year when there is good harvest. *Phool-jagni* is performed when an old man dies.

This is a large scale function like a marriage ceremony, and relatives and friends, even from the neighbouring villages, may join. *Phool* or flower here means the soul of the dead person; and *jagni* means to awaken it so that it is satisfied and becomes a part of supernatural power.

The *Phool-jagni* starts with the beating of drums which is a sign to all villagers and neighbouring villagers to assemble. The youths and others from the area start collecting, uttering abuses and slang or vulgar words, and start dancing. As stated above, these utterances are supposed to propitiate the dead soul. On the rhythm of *dhols* (drums) and tune of flute they drink and dance in which women also join and sing. Men only dance but don't sing though they may hurl abuses.

A big stone or a log of wood (*Munda*) is brought and worshipped in their traditional manner. Some wooden images are also prepared from it or carved on the log of wood. Then this *Munda* is ceremonially installed like a God and at times small temple (*Mando*) is built over it. *Pooja* is offered on *Amavasya* day (moon-less day) following *Dussehra* and *Vaisakh* (i.e., the *Kartik Amavasya* in *Diwali* – the *Laxmi Pujan* day and the *Vaisakhi Amavasya* day) every year to this *Munda* which is followed with dancing and singing.

The Korkus spend lavishly on this *Phool-Jagni* function and may host two-to-three dinners. This function simulates the *Tervi* (the 13th day) which is observed by Hindus, and these days, many Korkus are also celebrating *Tervi* and dropping *Phool-Jagni*.

A ceremony called *Pitar-Miloni* (i.e., reunion of the soul of the dead with that of the dead forefathers) is also observed before *Sidoli* where turmeric is used. In Korkus there is no fixed period for performing these rites after burial.

FIVE

SPIRITUAL CULTURE

Gods and Goddesses

Like all other tribals, the Korkus too have many gods and goddesses. *Muthwa Deo* is a very important deity worshipped before any other God – before marriage ceremony or before going on a religious tour or before any other festival/ceremony. They worship *Nag-deo* (Snake-god), *Bagh-deo* (Tiger-God) *Khela Deo* and *Mahadeo* (Lord Shiva), Goddess and local deities.

Korkus are worshippers of Ravana – the King of Lanka, Meghnad and Kumbhakarna from Ravana's kingdom. At the time of *Holi* they sing songs in praise of Ravana which also mention that seeing Ravana in the costume of a *Jogi* (an ascetic) she was attracted and followed him. This 'She' is not specified but considering the legend of *Ramayana* it could be a reference to Sita. Ravana was also a worshipper of Lord Shiva, and so are the Korkus, and hence they link themselves with him. However, these days they also worship Rama.

Like *Mahadeo* and *Parbati, Hanuman* also figures in their religious folk-songs.

More interesting and intriguing is reference to rivers, the Ganga, the Jamuna, and Mathura which are from the North. This again supports the theory discussed earlier of their ethnic links with the Rajputs or Yadawas from the North during historical past.

Korkus are also nature worshippers. They worship *Dharti-Itamata* (Mother-earth), *Diya-Gomoj* (Sun-God) and *Rato-Gomoj* (Moon-God). They draw *Rangoli* (design drawn by using white stone powder), keep stones (quartz crystal) on it and worship Moon and Sun. *Diya-Gomoj* is the Korku word for the sun, which they consider as the supreme power in the Universe. According to a mythical story popular among Korkus, Sun and Moon were two brothers who went to take meals where a *Puja* was going on. Sun brought some cakes for mother but on way back he went to answer nature's call. Moon took the cake and reached his mother and offered it to her. Mother cursed the sun that he would always be burning while Moon will always be cool.

Two clan-gods are very common.

Rari – a Goddess is worshipped by some clans. A goat is sacrificed before it.

Bhusum – a God which is worshipped by some other clans by keeping it in foodgrains. Pig is sacrificed before this God.

They also worship fire and believe that it keeps the enemy away.

Kaptha – a bird (*Neelkanth* or *Blue Jay*) is respected and considered as a good omen.

The Nemad Korkus consider themselves as descendants of *Karkotaka* (a big mythological snake) and call themselves *Nagvanshi* (from snake-race). The Melghat Korkus believe that the earth rests on the head of a snake (a Hindu myth) and hence worship 'Snake God'.

They don't kill cows; and some even worship cow. However, they kill buffalo in a typical manner. The nose is cut and wounds are made on her body and it is then taken throughout the town. It is believed that when the fresh blood from the buffalo's body falls at various places on the road the deities are satisfied. They relish buffalo meat.

Muthua Gomöj (the village God), *Dongor Gomoj* (the mountain or jungle God) and *Harduli Gomoj* (the cholera God) are very often worshipped as local Gods. *Dongor Deo* is worshipped on *Dussehra* day and a goat, two coconuts, five dates and vermilion are offered.

Drawing upon the legend of the creation of mankind they also worship crow (*Kag Bhushundi* or *Kageshwar*).

They are horse worshippers, believing it to be associated with malevolent powers, probably having association with outside invaders who came on horses.

The Korkus are animists, but their animism is modified by a considerable admixture of Hindu beliefs and practices.[1] The 1911 Census gave figures showing more than half Korkus as Hinduised and even today most of them consider themselves as Hindus. Hindu influence is also obvious on their mythological folk-lore.

The various things used for *Puja* (worship) of Gods and at the time of festivals include turmeric powder, *kumkum, sindur* (vermilion), coconut, lemon, dates, wheat flour, chickens and cock, goat, *pig, khichadi* (a cooked recipe containing various cereals) and liquor.

The Muthua or Mutua-Deo Puja

Mutua-deo is a very important God for the Korkus. In every

village/town image of this God is installed and is like a local God or God of the village. It is worshipped before all other worships, festival celebrations, marriage ceremonies, etc., and as such it is a must for every village. It is generally created by collecting stones from a nearby river or stream and forming a heap of stones at some central place in the village. A pig and seven chickens are sacrificed before the heap and the Muthua Deo is created. Before all functions or ceremonies a goat or a pig or a chicken is sacrificed before this God.

A song in praise of Muthua-Deo, which is sung before the God at the worship before marriage is given below :

Am Kaja Muthua-Deo,
Ama liyen churni biliken,
Bhumka sana leka sabku,
Sana dhomna olewa;
Dava tite orpatiye, .
Jevana tite bola mendo buje.

Beginning of Eating of New Products

Every year when new harvest is ready and they want to start eating they worship Lord Mahadeo in their farms. Coconuts, dates, lemon, cock and flour of 1-1/4 kg. wheat is offered as *prasad*, the cock is sacrificed. Then they drink liquor and take meals and then bring the new grains home.

Festivals

The important festivals include *Rand-Bhave, Baisakhi* or *Bhavai, Jeroti, Dussehra* and *Holi. Diwali* is also celebrated but they call it a festival of Gonds.

Bhavai : This is a festival which is celebrated on the *Vaisakh-Amavasya* (Moonless day in the Hindu month of *Vaisakh*, i.e., some time in the later part of May) a week or so before the *Mriga Nakshtra* (which is associated with the first showers of rains).

A round brass tumbler of water (*Lota*) is first immersed in water and bubbles are allowed to came out. Then it is filled with water and tying a multi-layered piece of cloth on its mouth it is turned upside down and hung (*Ubadhandi*) and water does not come down due to pressure of air. Then it is again taken out and the cloth is removed.

At first when it is immersed it is observed as from which direction the bubbles came out, and it is believed that rain will also came from that direction. Similarly, they observe as to how many layers of cloth tied to the *Lota* became wet, and conclude that, that much intensity will be there in the rains.

For agriculturists this is an important festival. They don't sleep for the day and night because the whole year will also be sleeping. Some good work is done on that day, e.g., killing a rabbit etc. Sowing seeds may also start on this occasion. *Kheda-Deo* is worshipped by offering a cock-hen and *khichadi*.

Pipal tree and *Marukko-Sinj*, i.e., *Mahavriksha* (the great tree) is also worshipped. When the *Maruko-sinj* gets new leaves they believe that time for rains has come.

Rand Bhave : This is celebrated on the *Jeshtha-Amavasya* day (i.e., Moonless day in the month of *Jeshtha* – some time during May-June). This is a worship of Rain-god and of *Kheda*-God.

It starts with the *puja* of a frog. Then they bring a green bamboo which is also worshipped. This bamboo is later used on farm for driving the bullocks. Seeds are also worshipped. The Dandel songs are sung. These are the fore-runners for a good monsoon. This is called *Rand-Bhave*. After the first rain showers *Chikhala-Bhave* is celebrated to thank the Rain-God.

Jeroti : This festival is celebrated in *Shravana* – mostly on a full-moon day and is similar to *Raksha-Bandhan* of the Hindus. Sisters – mostly married – go to their brothers home and stay up to *Pola* festival. A simple cradle is tied to two stumps of tree (*jhula*) and the sisters sing songs praising the brother-sister relationship. Those who don't have brothers also sing expressing their sad feelings for not having brother. These songs are called *Dolar* songs. (*Dola* means rhythmic movements of body).

Dussehra : They celebrate *Dussehra* on a large scale but worship Kumbhakarna and Meghnad. Meat and liquor is consumed. Nose of a buffalo is cut and wounds are made on her body and the animal is made to move throughout the village so that the blood sprinkles every where. This is supposed to propitiate local deities. They eat buffalo flesh with relish. They dance and sing throughout night and don't sleep. In the morning *Dussehra* is celebrated.

Holi : *Holi* and *phag* are festivals connected with one and the same thing. The full-moon day or *Poornima* in the month of *Phalguna* (February-March) is the occasion for this festival. Their celebrations spread over a month. It starts before or at the time of *Holi* and extend about a week after *Holi*. The *Phagunai* songs are sung by men and women separately or together accompanied by *Timki, Dhol* and *Jhanj*. Vivid descriptions of nature are given in it. For demanding *Phag (Phag-Mangna)*, i.e., some gifts, they sing and dance in the most colourful manner and sing *Jamtha* songs and go from house to house starting from the important person(s) in the village. This goes on for five days after *Holi*, i.e., from *Poornima* to *Panchmi*. Their new year starts with *Holi*.

Holi is normally celebrated on a community scale. Big logs of dry wood are set on fire at some central place in the village and this is done at the hands of the *Mukhiya* (Chief). The *Muthua-deo* is at the central place in the village. After the *Holi* is ablized, the singing men on the rhythm of the tingling of bells, which are tied to their sticks, dance and move in a row to the *Muthua-deo* and again return to the *Holi*. Songs in praise of Gods and Goddesses, on the community life or describing beautiful woman, etc., are sung on this occasion by the men.

A he-goat is sacrificed and its meat is distributed to all in equal proportion.

On the *Rangpanchmi* day (second day of *Holi* when colours are sprayed on each other) a special programme of '*Jerry*' breaking is arranged. Normally *Puja* of Meghnath (i.e., Meghnad) is done before this celebration. A tall pole of smooth wooden stump, polished and made slippery by applying oil and redoxide, is erected and at its top one coconut, one-rupee and 25 paise and jaggery are tied to a small horizontal pole. The *Mukhiya* of the village is brought ceremonially by singing and dancing men and women. Then in his presence all women stand in a big circle around the pole with sticks in their hand and men stand behind women. They dance in rounds and sing the *Jerry* song. Men try to slip through the women's circle and climb and catch the coconut, etc., and women beat the men with sticks – dancing and singing continuously. Ultimately some men succeed and get the *Jerry*. This is a good combination of a festival, worship and a social game with music and fun. *Dhol*, flute and *Timki* are the instruments on which music is played.

Various *Holi/Phag* songs are given in this monograph. They wear new clothes and celebrate *Holi* on a grand scale for which they may borrow from money-lenders. Men, women, boys and girls drink liquor to the full and dance throughout the celebrations.

Bhumka/Parihar

Bhumka also called Padiyal or Ojha is an important person who acts as their traditional priest and gets priority treatment at all festivals, ceremonies, etc. He directs worships, tells bad and good omens, gives herbel medicines and also identifies and propitiates evil powers. All Korkus regard *Bhumka* as their traditional community leader and a socio-cultural guide. The village Patel (who may be a Police-Patel also) and *Bhumkas* are their traditional community leaders.

The priests of the Korkus are of two kinds – *Parihars* and *Bhumkas*. The *Parihar* may be any man who is visited with the divine afflatus or selected as a mouthpiece by the deity; that is to say, a man of hysterical disposition or one subject to epileptic fits. He is more a prophet than a priest, and is consulted only on special occasions. *Parihars* are rare, but every village has its *Bhumka* who performs the regular sacrifices to the village gods and the special ones entailed by disease or other calamities. On him devolves the dangerous duty of keeping tigers out of the boundaries. When a tiger visits the village the *Bhumka* prays *Bagh Deo* and makes an offering to the god, for warding off tigers.

The office of *Bhumka* is usually, but not necessarily, hereditary, and a new one is frequently chosen by lot, this being also done when a new village is established. All the villagers then sit in a line before the shrine of *Muthua Deo*, to whom one black and one white chickens are offered. The *Parihar*, or, if none be available, the oldest man present, then sets a paisa rolling before the line of men, and the person before whom it stops is marked out by this intervention of the deity as the new *Bhumka*.

The *Bhumka* usually receives contributions in grain from all the houses in the village; but occasionally each cultivator gives him a day's ploughing, a day's weeding and a day's wood-cutting free. The *Bhumka* is also employed in Hindu villages for the service to the village gods. But the belief in the powers of these deities is decaying and with it the tribute paid to the *Bhumka* for securing their blessings.

According to their own traditions the Korkus like so many other early people were born from the soil. They state that *Ravana*, the demon king of Lanka, observed that the Vindhyan and Satpura ranges were uninhabited and besought Mahadeo to populate them. Mahadeo despatched his messenger, the crow *Kageshwar*, to find for him an ant hill made of red earth, and the crow discovered such an ant-hill between the Saoligarh and Bhanwargarh ranges of Betul. Mahadeo went to the place, and, taking a handful of red earth, made images in the form of a man and a woman, but immediately two fiery horses sent by Indra rose from the earth and trampled the images to dust. For two days Mahadeo persisted in his attempts, but as often as the images were made they were destroyed in a similar manner. But at length of god made an image of a dog and breathed into it the breath of life, and this dog kept off the horses of Indra. Mahadeo then made again his two images of a man and woman, and, giving them human life, called them Mula and Mulai with the surname of 'Pothre', and these two became the ancestors of the Korku tribe. Mahadeo then created various plants for their use, the mahul from whose strong and fibrous leaves they could make aprons and head-coverings, the wild plantain whose leaves would afford other clothings, and the *mahua*, the *chironji*, the *sewan* and *kullu* to provide them with food. Time went on and Mula and Mulai had children, and being dissatisfied with their condition as compared with that of their neighbours, besought Mahadeo to visit them once more. When he appeared Mula asked the god to give him grain to eat such as he had heard of elsewhere on the earth. Mahadeo sent the crow Kageshwar to look for grain, and he found it stored in the house of a Mang named Japre who lived at some distance within the hills. Japre on hearing what was required besought the honour of a visit from the god himself. Mahadeo went, and Japre laid before him an offering of 12 *khandis* of grain, 12 goats and 12 buckets of water, and invited Mahadeo to eat and drink. The god was pleased with the offering and unwilling to reject it, considered that he could not eat food defiled by the touch of the outcaste Mang, and so Parvati created the giant Bhimsen and bade him to eat up the food offered to Mahadeo. When Bhimsen had finished the offering, however, it occurred to him that he also had been defiled by taking food from a Mang, and in revenge he destroyed Japre's house and covered the site of it with debris and dirt. Japre then complained to Mahadeo of this sorry requital of his offering and prayed to have his house restored to him. Bhimsen was ordered to do this, who agreed to comply on condition that Mula should pay to him the same honour and worship as he accorded to Ravana, the demon king. Mula promised to do so, and Bhimsen then sent the crow Kageshwar to the tank Dakdal, bidding him bring thence the pig Buddu, who being brought was ordered to eat up all the dirt that covered Japre's house. Buddu demurred except on condition that he also should be worshipped by Mula and his descendants for ever. Mula agreed to pay worship to him every third year, where upon Buddu ate up all the dirt, and dying from the effects received the name of Mahabissum, under which he is worshipped to the present day. Mahadeo then took some seeds from the Mang and planted it for Mula's use, and from it sprang the seven grains – *kodon, kutki, gurgi, mandgi, barai, rala* and *dhan* – which the Korkus principally cultivate. It may be noticed that the story ingeniously accounts for the sheds as it were an orthodox sanction on the custom of the Korkus of worshipping the pig and the local demon Bhimsen, who is placed on a sort of level with Ravana, the opponent of Rama.[2]

Magic and Superstitions

Magic

The Korkus have the same belief in the efficacy of imitative and sympathetic magic like all other primitive people.[3] Thus, to injure an enemy, a clay image of him is made and pierced with knife, in the belief that the real person will suffer in the same manner. If the clay can be taken from a place where his foot has made an impression in walking, or the image wrapped round with his hair, the charm is more efficacious. Or an image may be made with charcoal on some stolen portion of his apparel, and similarly wrapped in his hair; it is then burnt in the belief that the real person will be attacked by fever. Sometimes the image is buried in a place where it is likely that the victim will walk over it, when the same result is hoped for.

In order to produce rain, a frog, as the animal delighting in the element of water, is caught and slung on a stick; the boys and girls then carry it from house to house and the householders pour water over it. To stop rain a frog is caught and buried alive, this being done by a naked boy. Another device for producing rain is to yoke two naked women to a plough, who are then driven across a field like bullocks and stimulated and driven by a third naked woman.

In order to stop rain an unmarried youth collects water in a new earthen pot from the leaves and buries it below the hearth so that the water may disappear by evaporation and the rain may cease in the same manner. Another method is to send a man belonging to the *Kasada* sept – *Kasada* meaning slime – to bring a plough from the field and place it in his house. He also stops bathing or washing for the period for which a break in the rains is required, and the idea is perhaps that as the man, whose name and nature are mud or slime, is dry so the mud on the earth will dry up; and as the plough is dry, the ploughed fields which have been in contact with it will also become dry.

If a person wishes to transfer his sickness to another, he obtains the latter's clothe and draws on it with lamp-black two effigies, one upright and the other upside down. As soon as the owner puts on the clothe, he will fall a victim to the ailment of the person who drew the effigies.

In order to obtain children the hair of a woman who has many children is secured by a barren woman and buried below her bathing-stone, then the quality of fertility will be transferred to her from the owner of the hair. In order to facilitate child-birth a twisted thread is untwined before the eyes of the pregnant woman with the idea that the delivery will thus be made direct and easy; or she is given water to drink in which her husband's left leg, a gun-barrel, a pestle, or a thunder-bolt has been washed; it being supposed that as each of these articles has the quality of direct and powerful propulsion this quality will be conveyed to the woman and enable her to propel the child from her womb.

The Korkus have trust in omens.[4] It is inauspicious when starting out on some business to see a black-faced monkey or a hare passing either on the left or right, or a snake crossing in front. A person seeing any of these will usually return and postpone his business to a more favourable occasion. It is a bad omen for a hen to cackle or lay eggs at night. One sneeze is a bad omen, but two neutralise the effect and are favourable. An empty pot is a bad omen and a full one good. To break a pot when commencing any business is fatal, and shows that the work will come to naught. Thursdays and Fridays are favourable days for working, and Mondays and Tuesdays for propitiating one's ancestors. Odd numbers are lucky. In order to lay to rest the spirit of a dead person, who it is feared may trouble the living, five pieces of bamboo are taken as representing the bones of the dead man, and these with five crab's legs, five grains or rice and other articles are put into a basket and thrust into a crab's hole under water.

The occasion is made an excuse for much feasting and drinking, and the son or other representative who lays the spirit works himself up into a state of drunken excitement before he enters the water to search for a suitable hole. The fat of a tiger is considered to be an excellent medicine for rheumatism and sprains, and much store is set by it. The tiger's tongue is also supposed to be a very powerful tonic or stimulating medicine for weak children. It is cooked, pounded up and a small quantity administered in milk or water. When a tiger has been killed the Gonds and Korkus will singe off his whiskers, as they think this will prevent the tiger's spirit from hunting them. Another idea is that the whiskers if chopped up and mixed in the food of an enemy will poison him. They frequently are reluctant to touch a man who has been injured or mauled by a tiger, as they think that to do so would bring down the tiger's vengeance on them. And in some places any Gond or Korku who touches a man mauled by a tiger is put temporarily out of caste and has to be purified and host a feast on re-admission.[5]

Superstitions

The Korkus have many superstitions. For good and bad omens they consult the *Bhumka, Parihar/Padiyal* or *Ojha* which are names for the same post. Gods or evil spirits are then propitiated.

If a women is not bearing a child, the *Bhumka* is consulted. He is also a medicine-man. He diagnoses by examining pulse, nerves, etc., and may administer herbal medicine. If this does not work, *mantras* are chanted and worship of particular God is also performed, goat or chicken is sacrificed. If the woman conceives, again worship is offered and animals sacrificed.

They have *mantras* even for warding away wild animals. A man from Dharni reported in confidence to this author the following *mantra, 'Mukhya Sulur Gulur Peeu Shankar Savvaren'*. If you see a tiger and chant this *mantra*, the tiger will get aside and go away.

The pipal tree is worshipped because it is believed that *Daito Baba* lives on it.

When *Peesa* (Demon) catches a man, he is to be propitiated with a cigar (*Chilam*) of *Ganja*.

Even behind the worship of the dead forefathers, apart from respect, the idea of worshipping their spirits does exist. The *Sidoli/Phooljagni* function is also supposed to propitiate the spirit of the dead man and to give him peace.

With the spread of education the superstitious beliefs are declining though very slowly.

Astronomical Knowledge of Korkus

The Sun and the Moon are most important Gods for Korkus. Sun is called *Diya-Gomej* and Moon called *Rato Gomej*. The ancestors of the Korkus must have had good study of the stars and their effects. This can be concluded from the following beliefs held by them.

In *Vaisakha* (May) a round well-like circle of numerous stars is formed in the sky right above the head which is called *Semiya Bavdi* by them. One or two stars in the circle are more shining. This circle is considered as an indication of rains and they start preparations for sowing.

The seven-star configuration–which we call as *Sapta-Rishi* (Seven Hermits) is interpreted by them as being a golden cot – '*Soneki Khatiya*' with a thief entering to steal it (the three stars in a line). During night they find out the time from these seven stars.

When there is a circle around the star they say that all Gods are sitting in a *Panchayat* and a meeting is held to take some decision. If the rising moon of the 2nd day (*Beej*) is slightly inclined to west it is a sign of rise in prices and hence they sow more cotton (being a cash crop) which will help them to face the rise in price-line.

Churiyafeel – or star with a tuft of hair (*tail*), i.e., Tail-star – is considered indicating bad omen which brings calamities.

Suko or Venus is considered like a clock, because when Venus appears they say the day will break. Till the star goes down on the west the bullocks graze in the forest and then return to village.

Falling of stars is considered a bad omen. When clouds cover the whole sky and a sound of wind – like '*Ghoom-Ghoom*' – comes, hailstorm is sure to follow.

The Galaxy (*Akashganga*) is called *Raagli Kora*. They say it has two streams or branches – one of the father-in-law and the other of the daughter-in-law, because the daughter-in-law will never come before her father-in-law.

While taking meals one should not face southwards and while sleeping the feet should not be towards the south, as the south is not considered auspicious. While worshipping God the face of the worshipper should be to the east.

Moon, Sun, Earth and Fire are worshipped. The Sun is the supreme

God for them. Figures of Sun and Moon are drawn on earth by using power of calcium rock crystals (*Rangoli*) on which a quartz stone is kept and worshipped. Eclipses are interpreted as Demon's grasp over Sun and Moon and to relieve it they sing *bhajans*. *Mantras* are recited during ecclipse and sharpening of weapons is also done during this period.

This knowledge about stars, which combines observational facts interpreted in their own way of comprehension and mixed with popular superstitions, indicates that without any scientific aids they could think and draw conclusions about the Universe in the sky.

REFERENCES

1. Drake, John, (1914). Kurkus, in *Encyclopaedia of Religion and Ethics*, (Ed.) James Hastings VII, p. 761.
2. Russel, R.V. and Hiralal, (1916). *Tribes and Castes of the Central Provinces of India*, vol. III, pp. 551-53.
3. *Ibid.*, p. 563.
4. *Ibid.*, p. 564.
5. *Ibid.*

SIX

POLITICAL AND SOCIAL INSTITUTION

Political Organizations/Institutions

Among the *Korkus* the Patel – also referred to as Police-Patel – and the *Bhumka* (*Pujari* or priest) are the two important leaders of the village. The *Sarpanch* of the *Gram-Panchayat* also is a person whose name is included in the chiefs. However, this post is an innovation after democratic decentralization and the Patel and the *Bhumka* are the traditional chiefs getting respect and precedence in any socio-cultural matter.

There is no regional organization of the Korku community. In fact, a typical feature of this tribe is the lack of any hierarchical structure and absence of a chief for their tribe. Traditionally, it has a horizontal, federal set-up with only a village chief and no central power to control it.

Their Rajput Chieftains

Their kings were Rajput kings whose households are no more in existence. The Susarda jagir was under these Rajput kings with 12 villages in it. They had a fort at Kot (Chikhli) which is in a dilapilated form on the banks of the river Tapi on Madhya Pradesh border. The *Chavdi Panchayat* was under them. However, there are now no remnants of Rajput kings or kingdom and in the immediate past there were no rulers or traditional chiefs. It is likely that during the long past the Rajputs invaded the Korkus, had their kingdom at Susarda or at Kot and collected regular revenue from Korkus without establishing any formal political organization over them. One interpretation of the Korku worship of horse as a malevolent power has been related to some old-time terror associated with incursions of war-like foes. This may be linked with the invasion by Rajputs who came on horses, settled at some places and caught hold of some Korku groups who practised brigandage, raided the low-lying plains and from the loot paid the ransom to their Rajput chiefs. These Korkus were known as the Movasi Korkus and were held in high esteem among the Korku sub-castes. Movasi means a troubled country which may in turn mean that the Movasis were troubled by the invasion of the Rajput chieftains and had to work under their suzerinty, practise brigandage – which, in tribes, is a profession of high esteem – and pay regular *Khandani* or ransom to the Rajput chiefs. This may be supported by the ethnic relation with the Hill Korwas who also had Baghel Kshatriya chiefs who, in fact, were intruders and the Korwas also practised brigandage. (For details see author's monograph on Hill Korwas.) The Hindu influence which is discussed elsewhere in this book can be traced back to this Rajput influence. However, one thing is clear, that the then Rajput kings did not establish any particular social or political organization but were just content with the regular amounts they got and with their jagir. With their extinction, the Korkus were left with local village chieftains only. The reference of the Ganga, the Jamuna, Mathura, etc., and the worship of cow which is not original in Korku religion can be traced back to the erstwhile Rajput influence.[1]

In the erstwhile Central Provinces and Berar – now in Madhya Pradesh and Vidarbha region of Maharashtra – Rajput dynasties were ruling in Jabalpur from the 6th to the 12th century, in Seoni about the 6th century, in Bhandak near Chanda (now Chandrapur) from an early period as well as at Ratanpur in Chhattisgarh. From the 12th century they disappeared and there is a blank till the 14th century or later when Gond kingdoms were established at Kherla in Betul, at Deogarh in Chindwara and at Garh Mandla including the Jabalpur country and at Chanda, 14 miles from Bhandak. A group of Rajput chieftains from Jabalpur or Chhattisgarh could have made incursions on this Korku region, and might be paying a part of their revenue collection to their lords at Chhattisgarh. However, after the extinction of the Rajput chiefs in 12th century from Chhattisgarh and Jabalpur the Rajputs at Susarda lost all their support and became exinct; the Korku region remaining under their traditional local Patels.[2]

After the Chalukya kings, the Yadav kings of Deogiri ruled the north and they ruled over Berar including Amravati district and Achalpur, which is now a *tehsil* headquarters on the plains just adjoining the mountainous Melghat, was their provincial capital. The Yadavas – who were Hindus – ruled from 1189 to 1312 till their last king Shankar Deo was killed by Malik Naib and he annexed the Deogiri empire which included the Amravati district and Achalpur as well as the Melghat area, thus bringing the whole of Korku region under Mohammedan rule. At the end of 1316 Alauddin Khilji died and Malik Naib was assessinated and Harpal the son-in-law of Ramchandra, again seized power at Deogiri and ruled for some time but by 1318 Kutub-ud-din Mubarak Shah attacked and killed Harpal, and Amravati with the rest of Berar again passed into the hands of Mohammedans and remained under them till the treaty of 1853 when it was assigned to the East India Company. This explains the blank referred to above and explains the rule during the period after the 12th century, i.e., after the Rajput chiefs disappeared. The so-called Melghat Rajas of the six parganas, i.e., Makla, Dhulghat, Jamgarh, Mohokot, Khatkali and Rupgarh, who also claimed themselves to be of Rajput or *Chhatri* (Kshatriya) extraction, were in fact descendents of three adventures, viz., Bijairao, Gambhirrao and Garudrao, sent by Emperor Akbar three years after the close of Malwa war, i.e., in 1598, to populate these devastated parganas, the western and southern parts of Melghat *taluq*.[3] However, due to bad malarious climate they fled back to the plains but maintained their *Sanads*. In 1896, the British Government gavè *Sanads* to these Rajas as *Jagirs* but without hereditary precedence.

From all these historical sketches it is obvious that traditional Korku tribal organization had no centralized power to administer them and the only chief was the religious leader and the *Patel* of the village who might have maintained contacts with the Rajput rulers and later with the changing powers over the Berar or Vidarbha region.

The Profane Authority

The *Bhumka* and *Parihar* also wield power based on the supernatural powers which they may invoke or retrain from invoking for the protection as well as welfare of the community. The role thus adduces a status, and the influence brings about obedience. This is an instance of how the profane powers compel obedience and legitimatize the powers of the 'patron' in the tribal society. Fear of the 'unseen' is more potent and real as compared to the fear of physical punishment.

Social Institutions

There are no well developed traditional social organizations among them. The social institutions include family which is patriarchal and patrilineal but the women in general don't receive bad treatment. Marriage and religious institutions are ritualistic as described earlier.

Inheritance goes to the mother (i.e. widow) and the unmarried male children, the property being equally divided among them, and the daughters don't get any share.

The social relationship among the four sub-tribes simulating sub-castes of Korkus is based on equality, though the Goyaras are treated as low-castes and the other sub-castes don't keep eating as well as marriage relations with them. The Movasi Korkus are held in high esteem. But there is no rigidity, and relations are cordial. Marriage is exogamous but there are matrimonial relations between the three sub-castes, viz., the Rumba, Movasi and the Bondoya. The socio-cultural life is common to all.

Adoption of Practices from Outsiders

The Korkus have largely adopted many socio-cultural characteristics from the culture of the plains of the adjoining areas. Dress and food habits are significant. They even take allopathic medicines and go to government as well as private dispensaries at Paratwada and Achalpur.

Many have converted their sept names into surnames, e.g.,

Sept	*Surname*
Kasda	Kasdekar,
Movasi	Mavaskar,
Mara/Murirama	Morey,
Jambu	Jambekar

Some have even adopted outside surnames like Savarkar which sounds Brahminical.

Giving-up *sidoli*, they are now celebrating *Tervi*, i.e., the 13th day to satisfy the soul of the dead. Even in their marriage ceremony some adopt rice-throwing and the recitation of the *Mangalashtaka* (The eight sacred verses), etc., which are practised by the high-caste Hindus in the adjoining area. Gifts to the bridegroom are given in some marriages (like dowry) which is an antithesis of bride-price.

REFERENCES

1. Russel and Hiralal, (1916). *Tribes and Castes of Central Province of India*, III, p. 506.
2. *Ibid.*
3. *Ibid.*

SEVEN

THE KORKU DIALECT

The Korku dialect is from the Munda group of languages. The chief home of Munda languages was Chota Nagpur. Grierson also considers it as one from Kherwarian tradition. The following 14 dialects belong to Munda group :

1.	Santali	8.	Asuri
2.	Mundari	9.	Korwa
3.	Bhamji	10.	Korku
4.	Birhar	11.	Kharia
5.	Koda	12.	Juang
6.	Ho	13.	Savara
7.	Turi	14.	Gadaba

Thus, Korku is related to Santali of Kherwarian group of languages. It has only one sub-dialect, viz., Movasi.

The Dharni Tribal Settlement Report also considers Korku as a language spoken by Hindi-speaking Korkus. In some areas it is so much influenced and mixed with Hindi that some are tempted to consider it a sub-dialect of Hindi or a distorted form of Hindi. This only shows that Hindi and Nemadi have largely influenced it, next coming Marathi and Gujarati. Even some English words have entered in this dialect. However, it is evidently a separate Korku dialect.

Like many other tribal dialects in India the Korku dialect is also rich in folk-literature. It has no script and has an oral tradition.

Some words given in the Appendix I show the nature of the dialect. *Devnagri* script can be easily used to transcribe the dialect.

Structure of the Dialect

It has a richly developed phonetic system. Law of harmonic sequences affecting the law of consecutive syllables is observed. Consonants –

hard and soft – and the semi-consonants (a characteristic of Munda languages) are present. In words borrowed from Aryan languages, aspiration is dropped. This tendency of adding or dropping aspiration while borrowing words from other languages may be adduced to an overconsciousness on the part of the borrower to show that the word is properly pronounced.

Pronunciation

Pronunciations are broadly similar to Santali.

E	&	O	as (bone)
a	as	ai	as (table)
a	as	a	as (yes)

Deep gutteral pronunciation and an interchange of short and long vowels are common.

Class consonants are same as in Santali.

Influence of Marathi, the regional language of the neighbourhood, is also seen.

Nouns

Suffixes denoting animate objects and inanimate objects are used. This is similar to the Korwai dialect of the Korwas.

Words indicating genders are added to nouns. There are only two genders.

For example:	*Kon*	means	son
	Konje	means	daughter

Thus suffix '*je*' is added.

Numbers

There are three numbers, viz., singular, dual or double and plural. This also is a similarity with Korwai dialect. On this point the Korku dialect simulates Sanskrit.

For plural the suffix is '*Ku*', e.g., *Kor* – man and *Ku* – many, i.e., a community of men.

Case : Cases are often left un-marked. Like other Munda languages it does not possess anything corresponding to the cases of the direct or indirect objects.

The various relations of time and space are indicated by adding prepositions.

Adjectives

Adjectives don't change with gender, number or case.

Verbs

Direct objects are not distinguished but the indirect objects are distinguished.

Simpler conjugation than Kherwari is observed. Aryan languages have influenced the verbs in this dialect.

The number of subjects is indicated by adding usual dual and plural suffixes. No suffix is added if the object is an inanimate thing.

Active and passive voices are distinguished as in Kherwari.

Negative imperative is formed by prefixing *baki*, e.g., *baki* total – do not bind.

The dialect has separate terms for elder brother – *dada* or *dadu*, and younger brother – *boko*, also for elder sister – *bai* or *jiji*, and for younger sister – *bokoje*, but there is no term for brother or for sister in general. Similarly, Man - *Koro* or *Dota*, Woman - *Japai* (aspiratory, i.e., *Zapai*).

Now let us see some forms of verbs.

I was	*Ing tatak - dan*
You were	*Am tatak - dan*
He was	*Di tatak - dan*
We were	*Abung tatak dan*
You were	*Ape tatak dan*
They were	*Diko tatak dan*

be	*take*
to be	*takaba*
I may be	*Ing taku*
I shall be	*Ing dao-ba*
I should be	*Ing take Jadaren*

Verb

beat	*Munda*
to beat	*Mundaba*
beating	*Mundae*
Having beaten	*Mundae*

Present Tense

I beat	*Ing mundaba*
You beat	*Am mundaba*
He beats	*Di mundaba*
We beat	*Abung mundaba*
You beat	*Ape mundaba*
They beat	*Diko mundaba*

Past Tense

I beat	*Ing kumakane*
You beat	*Am kumakane*
He beat	*Di kumakane*
We beat	*Ale kumakane*
You beat	*Ape kumakane*
They beat	*Diko kumakane*
I am beating	*Ing munda lapken*
I was beating	*Ing munda dan*
I had beaten	*Ing munda daren*
I may beat	*Ing mundada*
I shall beat	*Ing mundej ba*

Future Tense

You will beat	*Am mundej ba*
He will beat	*Di mundej ba*
We shall beat	*Ale mundej ba*
You will beat	*Ape mundej ba*
They will beat	*Diko mundej ba*
I am beaten	*Ing mundyuba*
I was beaten	*Ing munda kane*
I go	*Ing seniba*

You go	*Am seniba*
He goes	*Di seniba*
We go	*Abung seniba*
You go	*Ape seniba*
They go	*Diko seniba*
I went	*Ing sen en dan*
You went	*Am sen en dan*
He went	*Di sen en dan*
We went	*Ale olen*
You went	*Ape olen*
They went	*Diko olen*
Go	*Ba, senie*
Going	*Senie*
Gone	*Senie*

Pronouns

Personal pronouns of the first person have two forms.

PRONOUNS

One excluding the party addressed	One including the party addressed
e.g., Personal – ing	ka . . . . .myself

First Person

Single	*Double*	*Plural*
(I) ing	(We two) *aling alang*	(We) *ale/abung*
(to me/of me) *ingya*	(of we two) *alinga alanga*	(to us/of us) *aleya abunga*
(I/me) *ing*	(We two) *ling lang*	(we all) *le bung*

Numerals : Numerals are counted in twenties, e.g., Upun is eighty.

DIFFERENT PRONOUNS

Ing (I)	*Iya** [1] (Me or ot me/mine)
Ale, abung (We)	*Aleya* (our/of us)
Am (Thou)	*Ama* (of the/thine)
Ape (You)	*Apea* (of you/your)
Dich (He)	*Dija* (of him/his)
Diku (They)	*Dikua* (of them/their)

1. * Iya — to be pronounced like Inya, i.e., with a nasal sound.

EIGHT

THE KORKU FOLKLORE

STUDY OF FOLKLORE

The community life of any population is reflected in all the acts and words of that community. These actions and words are reflected in their folk-literature which exists only in memory and finds outlet in spoken words. Thus, the oral folk-literature of a tribe is a spontaneous flow of the cultural norms and modes of behaviour, their physical life including environment, their likes and dislikes, their fears and inhibitions, their history and ambitions and their love and conflict. The spiritual and the profane aspects of life are intertwined in these expressions.

Types of Folk-lore

This oral expression is usually classified under the following categories :

I. *Folk Songs*

1. Sung by :

   (a) women
   (b) Men Mostly in dance-form
   (c) mixed

2. Ritual songs
3. Lulling songs
4. Love songs
5. Marriage songs
6. Festival songs
7. Songs for the worship of the dead

8. Tale songs
9. Game songs
10. Rhymes for children

Many or most of these songs are sung while dancing. Usually the whole village community participates in these dances. Tribals are accustomed to dancing and singing simultaneously and singing by sitting is not possible. Hence most of these songs can be best described as 'Dance songs'. These are not 'sung' but 'danced'.

II. *Folk-tales*

1. *Narrative*
   (a) Tale-songs
   (b) Stories

2. *Subject-matter*

   (i) Based on origin of the tribe/clan, etc.
   (ii) About supernatural powers/nature, etc.
   (iii) About Gods/Demons.
   (iv) About Bravery.
   (v) About the dead forefathers.

III. *Folk-stage*

The performing arts of the tribals are very rich and traditional attire, styles, make-up, decorations and musical instruments, etc., are profusely used. These are of the following types :

(i) Festival performances
(ii) Ritual performances
(iii) Historical events re-enacted
(iv) '*Tantric*' or connected with black-magic
(v) Martial type–displaying the unity of the tribe and fierceness against enemies.

IV. *Other Forms*

(i) Idioms and phrases

(ii) Quiz
(iii) Abuses and obscene/slang sayings, words, etc.
(iv) *Mantras*

Sources and Inspirations of Tribal Folklore

The sources and inspirations for folk-literature are mainly from the environment. The natural phenomena like the thundering of clouds, ripples of flowing river water, twittering and singing of birds, shrieks and roaring of wild animals, even the soft sound of leaves of trees – all provide inspiration for the flow of tribal literature. Hence, imitation is a most powerful source. Onomatopoeic forms are often present in their literature. The attires, colours, styles and movements in their art-forms are also adoptions or imitations from nature. The sources are thus internal to the total environment, and surprise, affection, joy and fear find expression in their folk-lore. The producer or composer of the folk-lore is often the community and the enjoyment and performance of the same is also on community level – there is no audience or spectator in real sense.

In some cases someone or a few may initiate or lead the performing or composing group and others repeat and even go on adding to what is provided by the leader as a starting point. Hence the so-called 'Communal authorship' exists but within it, there is occasionally an individual authorship or at least an individual initiative followed by communal contribution to the themes, words, rhythm and movement. Tribal composers are 'quick-poets' and they go on weaving ideas in words befitting the occasion at times repeating the old verses and at times composing new ones–though the musical form and style is maintained.

Absence of inhibitions in giving vent to emotions/sentiments and in use of words and experience of ecstasy are two more characteristics of tribal folk-lore and art forms. If the tradition dictates or occasion warrants an obscene phrase or action, neither men nor women will hesitate to express it freely and with pure joy without malice towards anyone. On the other hand the Korku folk-lore has specific emphasis on such abuses on certain occasions.

Animism and totemism are also reflected in their folk-lore. The astronomic bodies, the earth, trees, shrubs, animals, the visible and the invisible – all provide the subject-matter for their literature.

The folk-tales are usually attempts by 'the wise' to interpret the universal phenomena, to explain man's origin and particularly of their tribe. It also covers the tales of forefathers, their bravery, tribe's relationship with animals, the value and significance of Sun, Moon, Stars, Mountains, some birds, animals and even trees.

Almost as a rule, most of the tribal communities – irrespective of their ethnic origin – are worshippers of Lord Shiva (Mahadeo) and Goddess Parvati (Mata). There are also numerous local Gods and Goddesses. A rich mythology regarding the social ordering of their tribe by Lord Mahadeo is explained in many folk-tales.

The stories related to erstwhile chieftains, rulers, etc., are also known. Right from Rama and Krishna to Ravana and Kumbhakarna, and from Lord Mahadev to Rajput zamindar chieftains of Susarda – all find place in folk-tales.

Adoptions from other languages, cultures and assimilation in their traditional styles is also an important source. The subject-matter, symbols, words, composition and styles are also adopted. Singing of *bhajans* and use of *harmonium* or *lezzims* during singing/dancing is an example. Even the traditional attire/dress is giving way to the new five-metre *sari*, pants, shirts during dancing – when the younger generation participates in such dances. This may be called as an example of acculturation through introjection.

Continuity and slow change is thus a characteristic of Indian tribal culture, which is inevitably reflected in their folklore. Tradition is maintained and passed on to the new generation but with additions and new super-imposition, which are indicative of the dynamism of tribal ethos.

FOLK-SONGS

Attempting a Classification of Folk-songs of Korkus

A classification based on the available folk-songs of Korkus may be attempted as under :

1. *Festival Songs*

   (i) *Bhavai*
   (ii) *Jiroti*
   (iii) *Holi/Phag*
   (iv) Other festive occasions.

2. *Puja/Ritual Songs*

   (i) Auspicious or Puja occasions
   (ii) *Aarti*, Praise, usual prayers
   (iii) Birth – Names giving/Lulling songs
   (iv) Death rites – *Phool Jagni*.

3. *Love Songs*

   (i) Lover and beloved
   (ii) Marriage songs
   (iii) Siblings, in-laws

4. *Nature Songs*

   (i) Creation of Universe/Mankind
   (ii) Describing forest and animals

5. *Work Songs*

   While working in forest/harvesting/grinding, etc.

6. *Philosophical Songs*

   Advocating the futility of earthly life.

7. *Developmental Songs*

   New themes like education, etc.

The Korku term for songs is *Sirinj*. According to the style of dancing or occasion, etc., they name the *Sirinj* as under :

1. *Dandel/Danda Sirinj*

   Those in which the dancers (*Akhadi, Jiroti, Nagpanchami* and *Pola*) wield rods or '*dandas*' in hands.

2. *Dolar Sirinj*

   There is a *Jhula* (swing) hanging on a tree in the courtyard. These songs are sung by sitting on it; hence Dolar (rocking) songs.

3. *Horiyar Sirinj*

From *Holi* onwards – for five days these songs are sung. Hence called, *Horiyar*

4. *Gogolya Sirinj*

In *Chaitra, Vaisakha* – the boys (only) sing and dance for entertainment.

5. *Chacheria Sirinj*

This is sung by girls only.

Occasions for Singing Songs

The cultural life of the Korkus is replete with songs and dances. Men and women of all ages participate in it. It is community entertainment in a real sense. Important festivals, celebrations, events are the occasions for such dancing. Sporting turbans and traditional dress, ornaments, etc., they dance with vigour and enthusiasm which is still increased due to consumption of Mahua liqour, etc.

Dussehra, Jeroti, Bhavai – including *Rand-Bhave* and *Chickala-Bhave* – *Holi* or *Phag* are the festivals when many songs are sung and danced. Marriages and rituals for the dead, viz., *Sidoli/Phool-Jagni* are also marked with singing and dancing.

Installation of Gods, occasional *Pujas* and keeping of religious promises (*Navas*), sacrifices, ritual – like '*Khamm*' – are also the occasions for dancing.

Apart from festive occasions and ceremonies, even in their daily life singing and dancing has a significant place, e.g., while grinding, sowing or while cutting grass, songs are sung to forget boredom and these are in praise of women, nature or God, etc.

For lulling the child to sleep or for fondling it there are songs sung by mothers or sisters in their household.

Bhajans – particularly with Hindi influence from the Nemad side of M.P. – are also very common.

Musical Instruments

These include *Dhol* and Flute which are most popular and common. Then cames *Timki, Mridangam, Damru*, musical bells (*Ghungru*), Buffalo horns, etc.

Collection of Korku Folk-songs

Given below is a collection of folk-songs with meaning and comments wherever necesary.

This starts with songs connected with life-cycle rituals -- birth, death and marriage. They follow the songs showing love and affection between husband and wife, brother and sister, daughter and mother and the relationship of bride with her in-laws.

Next come the philosophical songs followed by *Puja* songs and the '*Khamm*' ritual-drama songs.

Then come festival songs – of *Holi/Phag* which include the tales of creation of Universe and mankind : *Bhavai* songs are sung after *Holi* songs. The *Jeroti* festival songs narrate brother-sister affection songs as referred above.

The next group is of work-songs, i.e., sung while doing work. These are followed by songs about Nature – prayer of rains, nature, natural beauty of a woman; other description of natural objects and forest.

Last song group is on social change and development, i.e., on education and conceptualization of the changing times.

In all these songs, the impact of Hindi   particularly Nemadi Hindi – is obvious.

Birthday Songs

Char Khut, Char bhawan
Rama Thakur rekha dale //
Pancho mahine ka loi
Nau mahine ke balak,
Sone ki thali
Ange dhulaya //1//
Sone Ke Zula Zulaya,
Aankh Ke diya, Hatha Ke Palana,
Our godi ki palaki,
Zula Zulaya. //2//

Tere Maane Mishri Dudh Pilayi
Ga, ga, geet sunai
Zula Zulaya. //3//

[O, child! Rama Thakur (Shri Rama) has given you life. In the fifth month you got blood, in the ninth month you came to this world. Mother gave you bath in golden tub and gave golden cradle for sleeping. Her eyes were lights and hands became your palanquin. She gave milk mixed with *Mishri* (sugar crystals) and she sung songs for you.]

Eh, dossoni, Eh dostin :
Aamni do ss do //
Cholaj ghar aave
Aamne do ss do //1//
Eh, Maina, Eh, Maina
Ja beta,
Aamne do·ss do //2//
Ghar laya tere roke re,
Aamne do ss do //3//

A lulling song to silence the child which has less of meaning but more of ryhthm. (O friend, O Maina please go, the child is crying, etc.)

Lulling Song

1. *Gai dodu re, Gai dodu re,*
Beta soja re,
Rona nai //
Gai dudhu re, Gai Dudhu re,
beta Soja re,
Rona nai //1//
Mayo aaya re
Rona nai //2//
Bapo aaya re
Rona nai //3//
Maya aayo re
dudhu layo re
Rona nai //4//

[Beta (child) don't cry, sleep. Your mother is bringing cow-milk for you. Your father has come, mother has come. Don't cry, sleep.]

2. *Aama ye baba*
   Sage ba takra Ro s s Ro s s Ro //
   Katam ko boko,
   Katam ko boko
   Ro s s ro s s Ro //1//

(A rhythmic song for lulling children in cradle. The words are changed as per fancy.)

Sidoli Songs

Elder men say:

Hele re aama dodo gande,
Sana lagito dodo gande. //1//

The terms used are vulgar and straight-way refer to male and female genital organs and hint of intercourse.

The elderly women give reply:

Goynama murda muwar,
Aam rongo Kende muwar ebe hone.

(They tease the men questioning their manly abilities).

These are vulgar questions and answers full of abuses and sex acts. Only elderly and married women participate. Girls don't participate in it.

Raja Rutu Jamaikula (Kui s s)
Raja Rambai Jamaikula (Kui s s)
Raja Lootmare Zogda Sune (Kui s s)

These are also vulgar words addressed by women to men during the dance sequence.

Marriage Songs

When the newly married couple starts for going to the bridegroom's place the ladies on the bride's side sing this song :

I

Raini ma Raini Buru Raini
Raini Itang Kuva Lage

Soneki Chumdi Rupiyeka Ghada
Kisan li Ladli,
Kaun Jai Pani Bhare //1//

Apno Ra Duda Veta
Kisan Konji Ki Chij Bole
Kau Jai Pani Bhare //2//

Tuta Mendoki Manji Maya Do s s Do
Iyan Jugnu Dharnise Gaja Aave,
Pani Bhare //3//

(This dear daughter of the farmer whom he loved very much is now going to the well with a cushion of gold on her head and a silver pot for water kept on it.)

In Indian culture a metal-pot (*Ghada*) full of water is an auspicious sign in all tribal as well as non-tribal communities. Hence, the description which is in tune with the general cultural attitude and tradition. The golden cushion and silver pot indicate blessings of the singer that she will have plenty of earthly pleasures in her new household.

Bride's Father : (my) daughter has been married and has gone in the household of a rich person whose house is half full with gold and half with silver.

Gangulya Gangulya Do s Do s s Maa
— *Gangulya Ka Do s s Maa* ....
Gangulya Go Maya Gangulya
Do – Maya Inje Tokhe ....

Konje Tore Maya Aam Do do s s Do .... //1//
Konje Log tore Maya Do s s We s s
Konje Murto Do Do s s Do ..... //2//

Bridegroom : I have not yet seen the figure of the girl (bride) but huge money has been taken from me for her (as a bride-price.)

Go s Go s s Do s Rani, Go s Go s s Do Rani,
Gangula Gadan Koko Ga Kadoba,
Go Go Do s s Rani
Aa s mani Tankula Le Jawe He s s ndo
I s s ni Jali Kendawe
Go s Go s s Do Rani........ //1//
Bo s s Do Rani Bo s s Do Rani Baro
Hati Bodo
Rodo Bobo Do Rani Baro Hati
Go s s Go s s Do Rani....... //2//
As s s mani Iso Yendoy Yendo
Ini Paiso Le Khave
Go s Go s Do Rani........ //3//

[The bridegroom says, "O, my Rani (Queen) look! We shall go to the forest to catch fish, O, Rani let us go to the market, we shall take money with us and go to the market".]

Normally boys and girls settle their own marriages and they often meet in bazars. A young girl is addressed as Malan in such love songs.

Describing a girl, the boy says :

Loya Loya renge, Malan ke,
Jaisa bichhiya vaisa mol.
Loya loya renge Malan ke,
Jaisa pitra vaisa mol.

[When will Malan look beautiful? If she wears a *bicchiya* (an ear-ring). Again he repeats a question and says, if she puts on a *pitra* (an ornament) she will look beautiful.]

The song continues with the same question being answered containing various dress items and names of ornaments.

Another song addressed to a girl in bazar :

Soneki Chumli, repeki topli,
Malo wojaven, Malo muze namochari re.

Choja mana do hati Malo sename,
Malo muze nevle, namo-chari re.
Rupeki topli, sone ki chumli, Malo wojaven,
Malo muze namo-chari re.

Jirima do hati Malo senema - do malo,
Muze nevlo namo-chari re.

A silver basket is held on her (Malan's) head on a golden pad, and Malan (the girl) is asking me (the boy who sings this song) my name, being attracted.

He asks, Oh – Malan why do you go to market and ask my name? Malan is going to Jirima market and is asking my name.

Thus, the joy of the boy gets expression through this song.

The following song is a dialogue between a beloved and lover which is based on symbols from nature.

Hurula alam jodi bangonija,
Hurula balla Kuwada re;
Kesondi alam jodi ban dau do,
Kesondi balla Kuwada re.

Murula fagun maina doginjaja,
Kesondi balla Kuwada re;
Kesondi Iya bana bangon do
Kesondi balla Kuwada re.

[Oh, Hurula (lover) : If you marry me we will form a good couple, because I live in black-soil and you live in mountain.

Oh, Kesondi (beloved), our pair will not be a matching one because you are black (being from black-soil).

The beloved replies, don't go after my black complexion, but see me in *Phalgun* (month) when my youthfulness will bloom making me look beautiful.

The lover again says, I am a mountain-dweller and I cannot marry you but prefer to live in mountain.]

The parents and brothers and sisters of the bride are with a broken heart as the bride will be leaving their household. Hence, a song is sung before she leaves :

Kagda talan Chameli do beti,
Beti do tenya teka awa maya tiyayen.
Beti do tenya teka bai maya tiyayen,
Beti do tenya teka dai maya tiyayen.

[The fragrance of Jasmine flower leaves the paper (scented paper), so also you (bride) are leaving us, Oh bride you will now be away from your sister, brother and father, mother, etc.]

Eh Re Raja, Raj Bole
Akhatijo cheto Mena //
Rame gamo Raja Raj Bole
Or baja Bole,
Raja Raj Bole //1//

Eyananga Chata Bara
Miya Gheri to Yeja,
Raja Raj Bole //2//

Ama mandhe Dhaga Rani,
Ama mane dhaga Rani,
Yenjo Raja, Raj Bole //3//

Eh Raja, Eh Raja Aamke,
Kapile gayi chut Bhare
Yenjo Raja Raj Bole //4//

[O, Raja, due to the heat of *Chaitra* month I was late though I could heard the sound of *Baja* (Marriage musical instruments). Due to heat, I got giddiness and hence was late. My feet got heat burns on the road and hence I was late. Kapila cow was let loose and hence I was late though I could listen the music of marriage band.]

A Dialogue between a Lover and a Beloved

Akhani tijo cheto mahena Dhamu bochoba
Dhoke Choja Fulumare?
Akhani tijo cheto mahena Dhamu bochoba
Dhoke 'Baru' Fulumare.

Baruni Khopa Sali menan ja Dhoke.
Baruni Khopa Sali mare,
A mani mai Khat Ka Baka ma lanjo chofar tema sage
Dana nunuba bahana daki Dhoke
macho lien dokamaja

Akhani tijo cheto mahena, Dhamu bochoba.
Dhoke Choja Fulumare?

Akhani tijo cheto mahena Dhamu bochoba
Dhoke 'Cheto' Fulumare.
Cheti Khopa sali menan ja Dhoke

Cheti Khopa sali mare

Aamani Aaba Khat Ka Bakama lanjo
Chofar tema sage
Chilomni munu bahana daki Dhoke.
Epticha Meran daki re
Akhani tijo cheto mahena Dhamu bochoba
Dhoke Chejo Fulumare.

Akhani tijo cheto mahena Dhamu bochoba
Dhoke 'Jalwa' Fulumare
Aamani dai Khat Ka bakama lanjo
Chofar tema sage.

Oruoo Kokhla bahana daki Dhoke,
Khuti lien doki mare
Akhani tijo cheto mahena Dhamu bochoba,
Dhoke Choja Fulumare.

[The beloved asks the lover as to which flower blossoms in the hot month of *Chaitra* (*Chetu*). He tells her that the 'Baru', 'Cheto' and 'Jalwa' flowers blossom during *Chaitra* month. She then asks him to fetch those flowers for her. But he says that he is afraid of her mother, father and brother. She suggests that he should come under the pretext of drinking water, smoking *chilum* (smoking-pipe) and taking out grains from barrel, respectively, and secretly palce flowers at a place for her.]

The song, apart from being a love song also tells about the flowering season of certain types.

Girl departing after marriage

Kakdo talan Chameli do Beti,

Beti do tenya teka, aawa maya tiyayen.
Beti do tenya teka, Bai maya tiyayen.
Beti do tenya teka dai, maya tiyayen.

[Beti is like the fragrance of chameli flower on a piece of paper. As the fragrance leaves the paper in due course, you are also leaving us (going to bridegroom's place). Now you will be away from father, mother, sister, etc.]

Bridegroom to Bride after marriage

Bridegroom :

Chalo Rani Wo Chalo Rani
Chalo Rani .....
Apna Jana Door Hai,
Chalo Rani .....

Bride :

Dera Raja Dera Raja,
Mera Gehna Pahenungi
Chalo Rani ..... //1//

Eki Manjla Thevo Raja
Mere Mayase Milungi
Chalo Rani ..... //2//

Bridegroom :

Tere Maa se Kya Mile Rani
Mera Ghoda Nahi Thave
Chalo Rani ..... //3//

Mera Ghoda Dana Ghoda,
Mera Ghoda Nahi Thave
Chalo Rani ..... //4//

[After marriage the bridegroom urges the bride to accompany him to his home, but the bride asks him to wait till she puts on her ornaments and meets her mother. The groom tells her that his horse will not wait and why should she meet her mother. He urges her again to be quick.]

Indo Mali Re, Yendo Madi Re ....
Lakhopati Ghar me
Beti Ke Diyo, Indo Madi Re .... //1//

Aadha Chandi Re, Aadha Sona,
Lakhopati Gharme
Beti Ko Diyo Re, Yendo Madi Re .... //2//

(Daughter has been married to a rich (*Lakhpati*) man, whose house is full with silver and gold.)

Bridegroom to Bride

Haje ma jo Haje ma
Haje ma jo ladai lee re //
Inya me Ran Haje
ladai lee re //1//

Aama lee no sadi ko sadi
Eh, we redho ladai lee re //2//

Chokhra ten ma yewe Reja
Ladai lee re //3//

Inya me ja bara barso
Ba yado Haje wa
Ladai lee re //4//

(The bridegroom asks the bride to come to him by putting on the Sari given by him. The bride says she will not put on his Sari as she remembers her parents.)

Song addressed to the Bride

Aare mansat Renjo
Chare mansat Renjo
Be – sayo Rajaji //

Aaja man kakake
Bulavo Rajaji,

Aye man Bhayeke
Bulaye Rajaji Be – sayo Rajaji //1//

Kodo man nando
Bulayo Rajaji,
Bata man chita
Udayo Rajaji, Be – sayo Rajaji //2//

Sone ki Niwala
Khilaya Rajaji,
Rupaye ki Pyala
Pilayo Rajaji,
Pilaya Rajaji – Be – sayo Rajaji

[The bride is asked to come as Rajaji, i.e., bridegroom, is waiting for her. Your lover has come and is waiting to chat with you. He is ready to offer on a golden plate (some edible) and give drinks in silver glass. He is sitting and waiting for you.]

Husband and Wife Dialogue

Gagra Rita Hirnya pani Ku Jawn Re,
Mharo sadi gili, Hirnya Me nai Jawn Re //1//

Mharo Dhoti Perile Hirnya pani Ku jawn Re,
Mharo Dhoti gili Hirnya Me nai Jawn Re //2//

Mharo Sadi Perile Hirnya pani Ku Jawn Re,
Mharo Kamro dukhe Re Hirnya Me nai Jawn Re //3//

Mharo choli perile Hirnya pani Ku Jawn Re,
Mharo gagra Rita Hirnya pani Ku Jawn Re //4//

[As her *sari* is wet the wife requests her husband to fetch water as the water-pot is empty. To avoid work Hirnya – her husband – asks her that as his *dhoti* is wet how can he go? She tells him to put on her *Sari* and go. Then he tells her that his waist is aching and he cannot go. Then she asks him to put on her *choli* (Blouse) and to go.]

Husband says to wife :

Kari Zari muti Rani, Kari Zari Muti do ---
Chuja Sati do Rani, Aama Met da Muti Sendate joroyen,
Kari Zari Muti Rani, Kari Zari Muti do ... //1//

Aama Mai Bhi inj ka Rani
Aama Aaba Bhi inj ka Rani
Chuja Sati Aama Met do
Muti Sendate Joroyen
Kari Zari Muti Rani, Kari Zari Muti do ..... //2//

After coming to husband's house the bride shed tears as she remembers her relatives. Then he say :
(O, Rani, why are you weeping and shedding pearl-like tears from your nice eyes and from your nose? Now I am mother, father and everyone for you, so please don't shed tears.)

Kuthi Me to Chana Rani,
Kuthi Me to Chana.
Rani edi lige wo........ //1//

Raja Re Raja Mhara Rajo,
Raja Re Raja Mharo Raja
Mharo Matha Dukhe Raja
Me Kaisi Hedu re? ... //2//

Payali Me to Gehun Rani
Payali Me to Gehun Rani
Hedi lige wo,
Raja Re Raja Mhara Rajo,..... //3//

Raja Re Raja Mharo Raja
Mharo Hatu Dukhe Raja,
Raja Me Kaise Hedu Re...... //4//

[The husband tells his wife to take out *Chana* (Gram) from *Kothi* (Barrel), when she says, O, Raja, My head is aching, so how can I do it? Then he tells her to take out *Gehun* (wheat) in a *Payali* (i.e., the unit used for counting) when she says that her hands are aching so how can she do it.]

The song is continued to any length when resourceful singers go on imagining situations and the probable dialogues between the husband and wife.

Koke Aama Do, Rerangi, Koke re,
Rangi Sangu Aayo mare /

Chojoni bana do, risana koke re rangi
sangu Aayo mare /

Lehanga bana do, risana koke re,
rerangi sangu Aayo mare /

Chojani bana do risana, koke re,
rerangi sangu Aayo mare /

Chorgi bana do, risana koke re,
rerangi sangu Aayo mare /

Chojani Bana do Risana koke re,
rerangi sangu Aayo re /

The newly married wife is not talking with her husband so he tries to cajole her by saying "listen to the tunes of Rerangi (a musical instrument), I will bring clothes for you" He goes on adding items to the list and tries to persuade and please her.

To bridegroom

Jogi fate hai lodoni
Kaise le kaise le //

Mharo to Nand Ke Raja
Aamne to Kawana bade chale
Kaise le Kaise le //1//

Aamne tomne baran Singni
Mor sikne Nand ke Raja
Rani Nand chale
Kaise le, Kaise le //2//

[O, Jogi (Bridegroom) where are you going? This Nand Raja is going to his house (Bada).

The Rani (bride) is also going in Barat to the place of Nand Raja who is going like a peacock.]

Parting of the Sister and brother

Jiroti Se aye piu pola me chale
Here piu ronsathi man Zure -
Ayo wa Raja Jiu palango me sowe
Here Piu ransathi man zure.

[The girl had gone to her brother for Jiroti festival and had been at his place up to Pola festival (i.e., for about two weeks), She now remembers her lover – husband – and says that she longs for him while going to bed.]

Sister to Brother on her marriage

Aamani jari do katri inlimanja daĭ Mor
Iyani jari do katri raili dongor Behna Bocho.
Dewo to Dewo re Bhaiya, Nahi to
kuwari Beti ka wanwasi re,
Juggo ma Juggo re, wanwasi Bhaiya,
Sata ma juggo re, wanwasi re.

[The married sister asks her brother to give her Jari (Jari Saree) and bowl to her. The brother says he left it in the forest and hence is unable to give. She says, "if you want to give, give these things. Now she is going for penance to forest for seven births (i.e., going to husband's house which will be repeated in seven births.)]

This shows that going to the in-laws house is equated with going to forest for penance. Similarly the Hindu concept of getting the same man as husband in seven births is also reflected. She feels that unless the brother provides for her (*Jari, Katori*, etc.), it will not be possible for her to undergo the ordeal of staying in the husband's house along with the in-laws.

Danda Songs (Jiroti Festival)

Pani bhare chali Gauri, jai
Pani bhare chali //
Hare mano bhaiya re
Pani bharan chali jaiva re, //1//

Kuwalase Pani bharaye,
Gauri pani bhare chali jai //2//

Hare mano bhaiya re,
Pani bharan chali jaiva re,
Kuwalase pani bharaya
Gauri pani bhare chali jai //3//

Hare jara Jamuna se pani bharaye
Pani bharan chali jaiva re,
Kuwalase pani bharaya,
Gauri pani bhare chali jai

(She has gone to fetch water from well, O brother, she has gone to fetch water. She has gone to river Jamuna for fetching water.)

The brother is enquiring about his sister and he is told that she has gone for bringing water.

Tin pair titaraka kaisi chalaya //
Khari Gawan Dhabalu kaisi chalye,
Kaisi chalaye. //
Kuwan ka panghat gai re pori,
Kaisi chalaye //
Poriyoko Dekhakar Hans gai pori
Kaisi chalaye //

(How does she walk – like a tripod titar. How does she go after cow to the field? How does she walk? Looking at her the girls/boys laugh.)

Babu Ke Angna,
Chandano Ki Zad
Koyal Bole //

Koyala Bole Baba,
Koyal Bole.
Kale kala bole,
Baba, Koyala bole //1//

Kale Kala bole,
Andheri rat koyala bole //2//

[At Babu's (brother's) place there is a Sandalwood tree on which a Cockoo is uttering sweet tune. The black cockoo is singing on the dark night at his place.]

Sister to Brother

Aakhadi Ka Tyohar
Bhayya aai gayo re //
Aake Bhayya Moke lene Ko
Aao re.
Bhayya Aai gayo re //1//

Aakhadi Ka Tyohar
Bhayya aai gayo re
Aare Bhayya moke lene nahi
Aao re, aai gayo re //2//

Wegi Wegi aao bhayya
Meri ladni bhaini Oke
Lene aao re, aai gayo re //3//

(The sister is awaiting her brother to come and take her home for *Jeroti* festival. She says that the festival has came but brother has not yet come to take her home. O, brother come as early as possible to take your loving sister to her mother's house.)

Mother and her daughter

Mai O Mai Maro Mai
Nadipara Men Kanya Kunwari Hindo da bandhe //

Beti O Beti, Maro Beti,
Apna Aangena hindoda Beti Mati Jajo //

Asli Parote Rani O! Beti,
Nahi to kali Golan Che O //

(The daughter asks permission from her mother for going to the other side of the river where swings are tied to trees. Mother tells her that it is present even in their home and if she puts on jwellery she will look beautiful or else she will look ugly.)

Jimo beti pan bida jimo
Aao, Beti pan bida jimo
Dai, O, pan Bida Kaduwa na lage //

Aao mai Kaduwa na lage
Khas sasura pan bida Mitha na lage //

[Mother offers beetle to her married daughter. The daughter tells her mother that this beetle offered to her (by her mother) does not taste bitter but the beetle offered to her by her father-in-law and mother-in-law does not taste sweet (i.e., tastes bitter) to her.]

This song depicts the traditional in-law relationship in contrast to that of mother and father.

The married girl and her In-laws

Nikal wo jiji – Bai Baheru Bhai se Milane Ku ja
Me Kisi Niklu Bhai Baheru Devrana lagi Re Kiwad
Bulayo re Bambai Sonar kati liyo re sone ki kiwad
Nikal wo jiji – Bai Baheru Baba se milne ku ja.

Me kisi niklu baba baheru sesran lagi re kiwad
Bulayo re Makdai Sonar, Kati liyo re sone ki kiwad.

(O', jijibai your brother has come to see you, come out of the house. Jijibai replies, the golden door of my house is closed how can I come out? Call a goldsmith from Bombay to open the door. She is again asked to come out when she says 'the father-in-law has closed the door, call a goldsmith from Makdai and cut open the golden door so that I can come out.')

The song depicts the constraints on a married girl from her in-laws.

The song shows that they know Bombay and can think of a door of gold and an expert goldsmith from Bombay to open it.

The In-laws and Bride

Dudha hoy to de wo nanadu,
Dudha hoy to dewore — //1//

Kahe ki dudha nanadu tukhe deu wo,
Gayya Hoy to jungle nanadu,
Ghaisi Hoy to do bhan.
Kahe Ki dudha nanadu tukhe deu wo — //2//

[O', Nanad (husband's sister) give some milk. Nanad replies "How can I give milk when the cow has gone to forest and the buffalo has gone to ponds? So how can I give milk.]

This song denotes that a 'Nanad' is not helpful to her sister-in-law.

To Sister-in-law

Eh, Kelta Dedej Do, Bawan Aamni Aajema do
Kelta Dedej Do, Bawan Aamni Aajema do
Eh, Kelta Suban Zanzre kula burum Ken
Gawa Koran ten Bawan Boni Erage
Bore boboj do, Bawan Aamni Aajema do
Bore Suban do, Bawan Zanzre bana Burum Ken
Bawa Koran ten bawan Boni erage.

Their is jocular relationship between husband and his wife's sister (Kelta – i.e., Sali or sister-in-law).

[He calls her and says "O', Kelta we will go to bamboo forest to fetch Basole and, an old tiger is sitting there, we will return to town by road. O', Kelta we will go to forest to fetch Ber (Ziziphus sativus) and as an old bear is sitting there we will return by road to the town."]

Philosophical Song

Kali ja mati, Pila ja mati, mati Gerani
Lai Ja mata, Mati Gerani lai //1

Mati se to chandi Ghadaile, chandi Gerani Lai
Ja mata, mati Gerani lai //2

Mati se to Sona Ghadaile, Sona Gerani lai
Ja mata, mati Gerani lai //3

Mati se to tamba Ghadaile, tamba Gerani lai
Ja mata, mati Gerani Lai //4

Mati se to Pital Ghadaile, Pital Gerani lai
Ja mata, mati Gerani lai //5

[The earth/soil is black and yellow. From the black-yellow soil is found silver, gold, copper (*Tamba*), brass and all these precious metals are again returned to soil. Thus, this mother earth gives birth to all precious and lower metals and ultimately they fall back to her.]

The theme points to equality of origin and the fact that all return to dust. Thus, it is a philosophical song.

Moreover, it also shows that the Korkus had knowledge about extraction of metals from earth.

Ram nam lena jo Maina Ram nam lena
Ram nam lena jo Maina Ram nam lena //

Chun Chun Kankar ka Mahal Banaya
Ye *Mahal tera ki mera, O Maina Ram nam lena* //1//

Had jale jaisa jungle ki lakdi,
Bal jale jaisa ghansa Re,
Bala Ram nam lena,
O, Maina Ram nam lena //2//

Kawadi Kawadi maya jodi,
Jod ke fir Bhi kam me no aawe re,
Ram nam lena,
O, Maina Ram nam lena //3//

[O' Maina, you have collected stones after stones and constructed your house but whose house is it? Is it yours or mine? Better you utter Ram-Nam (Ram's name).

O' Maina, the bones burn (after death) as if it is wood from forest and hair burn like dried grass. Hence it is better to utter Ram-Nam.

O' Maina, you amass wealth by miserly savings (*Kawadi* – the old lowest unit of money) but it could not be of any use (you have to die), hence, it is better to utter Ram-Nam.]

This is a philosophical song. The theme is about surrender to the God and non-possession of earthly pleasures. It also shows the impact of 'Ram-Nam' though originally they are Ravana worshippers. When Ravana is worshipped – gold, silver, diamonds, etc., are referred to, but when Ram is remembered, it is followed by renouncing of earthly pleasures.

Puja Song

Haro Nilo Bans Ka Mandava Re
Baba Maro,
Haro Nilo Bans Ka Mandava Re//

Mandava me jode nariyal tangi Raya ki
Babu maro, Haro Nilo Bans ka Mandva Re//

[The shade (Mandap) is of green, blue bamboos. Coconuts are hanging from the roof of the Mandap. O, Babu, this is a Mandap of green and blue bamboos (for worshipping God).]

Harigali van me thara
Badi re, Bagicha Ram
Harigali van me, thara Chabutara Re //
Chabutara ke Aaspas limbuo Manaye Ram
Harigali van me thara chabutara Re //

[A religious promise is fulfilled by offering a Lemon near the altar (*Chabutra*) of the God in the green forest.]

This song is sung and can be continued by substituting names of Gods and offerings.

Ravana's Aarti (Puja Song)

Aarti ma Aarti Bai
Chojama Aarti do //

Chojama Aarti do,
Raja Ravana ke Aarti le //
Sone ke Aarti Bai,
Rupe ki Bari Bai,
Rupe ki Bari Bai,
Raja Ravana ke Aarti le //

Ye Sali Ko sadi de,
Bai Hira moti Perile,
Hera Moti Perile,
Raja Ravana ke Aarti le //

Aarti Ma Aarti Bai,
Chojama Aarti do,
Chojama Aarti do,
Raja Ravana ke Aarti le //

[O, lady (Bai) whose *Aarti* are you doing? The lady tells that it is king Ravana's *Aarti.* The *Aarti* is of Gold and the wick, is of silver, the lady has put on new *sari* and has diamonds on her body; and this lady is performing *Aarti* of King Ravana.]

Korkus are worshippers of King Ravana and though they now worship the other Hindu Gods, this *Aarti* testifies to their original links with distant past.

Ravana Song – Dussehra Day

Lanka Ravani Jugi tau ten Olen Joy
Lanka Ravani Jugi tau ten olen .... *//1//*

Lanka Ravana Jugi Jodama Doyana Joy
Lanka Ravana Jugi tan ten olen .... *//2//*

Lanka Ravana tika Thenga Doyana Joy
Lanka Ravana tau ten olen .... *//3//*

Lanka Ravana Chunuka Chingi Doyana Joy
Lanka Ravana tau ten olen. .... *//4//*

Lanka Ravana danda Zuli Doyana Joy
Lanka Ravana Jugi tau ten olen .... //5//

[Rawana came with *Danda, Punji, Painjan, Jholi* and *Tika* and looked very impressive as a *Jogi*, and being fascinated towards his personality 'she' went along with him. (Who is 'She' is everybody's guess work!]

This song sung on the Dussehra day very much establishes their faith in King Ravana of Lanka whom they traditionally consider as their ancestor (*Ravan-banshi*) and King.

Before marriage they worship their Muthwa God and *Puja* is performed. The following two songs are sung at the time of *Puja*.

1.
Am Kaja Muthwa-Deo,
Ama liyen churni biliken.
Bhumka sana lela Sabku,
Sama Dhomna Olewa.
Dawa tite orpatiye,
Jevna tite bola mendo buje.

2.
Bhumkari Bhumkari,
Kharik, Limbu Pujanwalo Bhumkari,
Bhumkari, Nariyal, Sindur Pujnewalo Bhumkari,
Bhumkari, Kajal, Kunku, Pujanwalo Bhumkari,
Bhumkari, Murgi, Bakra Pujanwalo Bhumkari,
Bhumkari, Daru, Khichda Pujanwalo Bhumkari.

As compared to the first, the second song has many Hindi words. In this song the Bhumka or the priest who performs *puja* with various articles like coconut, *Sindur* (Vermilion), *Kumkum*, cock, he-goat, liquor, *Khichdi* (a mixed recipe) is praised.

Ganga Jamuna bhando laire Khilau,
Mathura Nangar Suwano Lal.

Sab devta ko Muthwa balore Ram,
Mathura Nangar Suwano Lal.
Hath jode re woke paya palore Ram,
Mathura Nangar - - - -
Sab devatanse Mahavir balore Ram,
Mathura Nangar - - - -

Hath jode re woke paya palore Ram,
Mathura Nangar - - - -
Sab devatanse khalkya balore Ram,
Mathura Nangar - - - -
Hath jode re woke paya palore Ram,
Sab devatanse Devi balore Ram
Mathura Nangar - - - -
Sab devatanse Mahadeo balore Ram,
Mathura Nangar - - - -
Hath jode re, woke paya palore,
Mathura Nangar Suwane Lal.

Thus, this song is in praise and prayer of Muthwa Deo, Mahavir, Khalkya, Devi and Mahadeo – the different deities worshipped by them.

Khamm

Kham is a ritualistic dance-drama performed from Ganesh festival (*Bhadrapad Chaturthi* to *Anant Chaturdashi*) and may be performed up to *Kartik Ekadashi*. However, if some took religious vow it may be performed any time up to *Ekadashi* or during *Diwali* festival

A wooden post (Kham or Khamm) is erected at the centre and on its upper end is fixed a wheel of bullock-cart. This structure represents the *Sudarshan Chakra* of Lord Krishna. Only men participate in this dance. Men put on *sarees* and perform the role of women. Songs regarding Rama-Laxman are also sung during this dance. Two groups participate in dancing and while one group initiates the other follows it. To start with they are in the *Vilambit laya* (slow pace) and then they pass on to *Drut laya* (fast pace). The songs are mostly based on Lord Krishna but names of Lord Ganesh, Lord Mahadeva, Goddess Parbati also follow :

Wari Wari Wari Mera Ganpati Deva,
Wari Wari Wari Mera Ganpati Deva //

Pahale manao Ganrajko,
Wari Wari Wari Mera Ganpati Deva //1//

Mata teri Parvati, Pita Mahadeva,
Wari Wari Wari Mera Ganpati Deva //2//

(O! Lord Ganpati, you are great and I worship you first. Your mother is Parvati and father is Lord Mahadeva and we worship them. O, Lord Ganesh you are great.)

They go on adding names of deities and can go on singing for any length of time.

Kanhaiyalal tune mhari ghagaraphode
Kanhaiyalal tune mhari ghagaraphode //

Etpar Ganga, Etpar Jamuna
Bichame Jamuna Bharaye, Nandlal
tune mhari ghagaraphode //1//

Jamuna ke neer tir, gauva charaye,
Bichame Sakhiya nache, Nandlal,
Tune mhari ghagaraphode //2//

[Oh, deer Kanhaiya (Krishna) you have broken my water-pot. On one side is Ganga and on the other is Yamuna (rivers) and Yamuna is in spates and O, Kanhaiya you have broken my water-pot.

On the banks of Yamuna (your) cows are grazing and in the midst the girl friends are dancing, O Nandlal (son of Nand, i.e., Krishna) you have broken my water pot.)

Holi/Phagnai Sirinj (Holy songs)

Nemo – maryo tere ban me,
Nim – maryo tere ban me //1//
Nim maryo tere pas,
Wo Chaliyo, dharni-ke lal
Loot liyo re
tere Ban me //2//

(I am lost in your forest, I am coming to you, O, friend, dear son of the earth, you have looted me; I am lost in your forest.)

Question-answer pass-time

Ye kabutar
Kisane mare //
Jaduse mare to
Kankarse mare
Kisane mare //1//
Ye kabutar
Kisane mare ---

This is a jocular question-answer type song for fun-making.

(Who killed the '*Kabutar*', and whether it is killed by magic or by stones? This goes on with different ideas.)

Holi Ke Re - Ronge
Bira - re Hanuman //1//
Kinija galko A Aado Dariya
Bira - re Hanuman //2//

This is in praise of Lord Hanuman who is brave and who jumped over the ocean.

Ram aur Lachaman Ye Dono Bhai,
chale wo Ban ko Nikale //
Aage Aage Ram chale,
Piche Lachaman Bhai,
Bichame chale Sita Maiya //1//

This continues and all important events from *Ramayana* are added to the song.

Hari lo le chalo
lo le chalo //

Uranai para lo
Base Katai lo
Hari lo le chalo //1//

Puranai para lo
Base katai lo

Holi ka Danda gadai lo
Hari lo le chalo //2//

This is sung by men when they go for cutting bamboo and wood for *Holi* – Let us cross Purna river and cut bamboo for our Holi. They usually bring 5, 7 or 9 bamboos for *Holi*.

Bakshis Song

Dego mayo re, mayo re //

Mayo re Jamadarna,
Dego Mayo re,
Mayo re, Mayo re //1//

Nandya Go Mayo re.
Dafedarna Dego mayo re
Mayo re, Mayo re //2//

The girls ask for *Phag*, i.e., *Bakshis* for *Holi*. They say *Jamadar/Dafedar* (i.e., officer or great man) I have come to you for getting *Phag*, please give us our due.

Holi Love Song

Nimbodi ke, saile Balema,
Limbodi ke saile Bole ma //

Saiyase Hoya Bharisa,
Balema Limbodi se,
Bole ma //1//

Saiyase Hoya Bole ma,
Limbodi se Saile
Bole ma //2//

The girl is talking to her lover. She is talking with her lover while performing *Holi*.

Story of Creation of Mankind

Hero ma Hero Waso malaye,
Seroma Seroma malkayro.
Hero Ka upar lal malaye
Heroya Jambu Morare /

Aagaso Dekhe kala chando
Dharetu Dekhe Dhuwa chale.
Hero Ka upar lal malaye
Heroya Jambu Morare /

Banaya Dane Surato Ban do,
Banayo Dane murato Ban do.
Hero Ka upar lal malaye
Heroya Jambu Morare /

Before creation, there was only a shade prepared from green bamboos and covered with green *Jamun* leaves and branches. In the sky the moon was black and the earth was covered with smoke or dew. Small fruits of *Jamun* tree were shining like small red beads. But there was no life – i.e., living creatures on earth.

The conceptualization of the Universe at the time of creation depicted in this song is laudable. Black sky and gaseous earth roughly simulates the scientific knowledge known today. *Jamun* tree seems to be of primitive existence.

The next song tells us how the Gods assembled to create mankind on earth.

Creation of Mankind (Holi Songs)

Herom Hera Baso Malaye
Serom Sera Man Kayro
Hero Ka upar lalo Malaye
Herya Jambu Mor Re........ //1//

Aagso Doge Dhuwandhar Do
Dharti Doge Kadapan
Abhyanindma Surato Ban
Abhyanindma Murato Ban...... //2//

Chetikoti Dewataku Dundiya Joda
Chatanni ja Suban Ken
Chetiskoti Dewataku Choja Mansuba tolemala
Kagaliya Masase usana mati
Aasini kule-bheja, kagaliya masa
Deriya tapun sene chalya Aafi Reja.

This is a traditional song explaining the origin of mankind. When 36 crore Gods assembled under a Banyan tree and decided to create mankind they sent the crow, viz., Kagbhusandji who had to fly a long distance for getting earth and had to lose its feathers also. Ultimately the crow succeeded in getting earth from Goddess 'Deemak Devi' (termite) who asked him to return the earth after the purpose is over. The crow agreed. The Gods then prepared idols of man and woman and poured life in them. The man is buried after death because the clay is to be returned as per promise given by the crow to Deemak Devi.

Aare bala aao, Purname phagun khele
Khele Maharaj;
Aao Purname Holi phagun khele

Rani Chali woke, Mayaka me O lal,
Raja chale, sasurai,
Are bala Purname phagun khele.

Ranike hatho-me Gulab ki Chadiya,
Rajaka hatho-me Kamal,
Aare bala Purname phagun khele.

Raja bethere houda, Rani bethere havadar,
Aare bala Purname phagun khele.

Maharaj (King) is playing *Holi* in Purna (River by name Purna) but rani (Queen) has started for her mother's place. Maharaj is also following her to his mother-in-laws' place. Rani has a rose flower in her hand while the Maharaj is having a lotus flower in his hand. Rani is sitting in a palanquin while Maharaj sitting on the back of elephant is playing *Holi* in Purna.

Bhavai Song

(*Rand-Bhave* and *Chikla Bhave*)

Potti Khede tu yeba,
to ye ba manaile //
Chikla bhave ye jeba,
Ye jeba manaile //1//
Baba Kade to yeba,
To ye ba manaile //2//
Chikla bhave ye jeba,
Ye jeba manaile //3//

(We are celebrating *Chikla Bhave* in our village, so you come for celebrating it.)

Rand-Bhave

Dedera mata pani de
Pani de //

Serom Serom, Serom Serom,
Jwarpala suki gayo re,
Pani de, Pani de //1//

Serom Serom, Serom Sarom
Dedara mata Pani de,
Pani de //2//

Rand bhave ye je ba lambe ko
Chikla bhave ye je ba lambe ko

Kodki kele lambe ko
Kutki Khede lambe ko
Chikla bhave ye je ba lambe ko //3//

(We are eating *kutki* and celebrating *Rand Bhave*.)

Baba sendaten da joran //
Baba Sendan Khali Bhurum Kendo

Baba Sendaten da joran //1//

Rabbit is sitting below paddy, let there be heavy rain so that the rabbit will come out.

Kutti ka lamba dekho de
De bai gana dekho de

Children dance with a pot of water and leafy branches on head and frog in it and sing the above song which has a vulgar connotation.

Gobin Mharo re
Sundar Gobin Mharo re //

Kayerisana Gobin Mharo re
Bada re sana Gobin Mharo re //1//

(This beautiful lady named Gobin is mine, wise old man, she is mine.)

Jago re jogi re
Nango re jogi ka joga //

Tone medeso aayo re jogi
Nanga re jogi nonga re jogi //1//

Surya madeso aayo re jogi
Nanga re deso ka jogi re //2//

Komor me to bhagawa Kapda
Khando me to Zoli,
Hatha me to lota, matha me to Chandan,
Nanga re jogi, nanga re jogi
Aayo re jogi //3//

[The *Jogi* (ascetic) has come who has saffron coloured loin cloth, a *jholi* on shoulder and *Chandan Tika* on forehead. From which country has this *jogi* come? Has he come from the country of sun God?]

Chandani Rato Kokdo,
Chandani Rat Kuldailala /

Bhawake Me to Bhawade
Beta Ho to Kunwa Khudaye /
Ekija tikaso mareoke
Ungalai Bhar Bhar panai re Lala/

(His son is so powerful that when he hit the earth with pick-axe, water comes out in one stroke. On a moon-lit night the boy did this act.)

Work-Song - While grinding on grinding stone

Chalo chalo wo Rani, wo kodi Mahadeva Makan me wo chalo
Hamku to matha me dukhi Aayo re Churasi Raja //1//
Nadiya nala bhi aayo wo churasi Rani //2//
Hatoja payochi topo wo Rani, wo kodi Hato ja paya chiti ye //3//
Chalo chalo wo Rani wo kodi kejali ja Bidraji Wanmeni
chalo wo rani wo kodi //4//
Mahadev Baba ka Makan, do chalo wo rani wo kodi
Mahadeva Makan me wo chalo wo dalaya Padyo //5//
Ekija Mahanabi Huyo re, churasi raja Ekija
Mahanabi Huyaji //6//
Duja Mahanabi Huyore, churasi raja Duja Bi Huyo ji //7//
Tinja Mahanabi Huyore, churasi raja Tin Mahanabi Huyo ji //8//
Char ja Mahanabi Huyore, churasi raja char
Mahenbe Huyoji //9//
Pacha ja Mahanabi Huyore, churasi raja Pacha
Mahenbe Huyoji //10//
Chhe ja Mahanabi Huyore, churasi raja chhe
Mahanabi Huyoji //11//
Sat ja Mahanabi Huyore, churasi raja satja Mahanabi Huyoji //12//
Aatha ja Mahanabi Huyore, churasi raja Aathaja
Mahanabi Huyoji //13//
Nawa ja Mahanabi Huyore, churasi raja Nawa ja
Mahanabi Huyoji //14//
Potoba Rajaji Padyo wo rani, kodi Mahadeva Baba se
Ful Patra bhi magyo ji //15//

The couple is going to the shrine of Lord Mahadeva. The husband appeals to wife– 'O, Rani let us go to the House of Lord Mahadeva'. She says 'O, Churasi Raja, I am getting headache. How can I come? He again appeals to her. She is walking for months and says one month is over, second month is over .... up to nine months. Then he tells her that as nine months are over let us go to Lord Mahadeva and seek His blessings for getting a son.)

This is sung by women in a chorus while grinding.

Nindena Aawore Bhabhi, Gorena Aawo.
Dongre Par Bara, Dongren Sarya Barase //
Nindena Aawore Bhabhi, Gorena Aawo.

[O, *Bhabhi* come for cutting grass and cleaning fields. Let us go on the other side of mountains, where it is raining. O, *Bhabi* let us go for grass-cutting (*Nindan*) work.]

Women's Song for Better Rains

(Chachariya Song)

(1) *Bhar joli ba Rani Barso Re s s Re*
Bhar joli na mai gharoli Re //

Bhar joli Aagas baba Bocho
Bhar joli Dhartine Aayam jolo
Barso re --- //1//

Bhar joli Hawa taku Khudua,
Bhar joli Doya Dagan tocho
Barso re --- //2//

Bhar joli gutaka Sugodan tocho
Bhar joli puri Niteka Baka
Barso re --- //3//

(The women say let there be heavy rains so that all pits and pots will be full with water.)

Similar Type of song (Chachariya song)

(2) *Goli Goli Goli ja,*
Kalya Nam Goli ja Bhitya Nam Goli //

Goli Aama patri Aakhei Ghataye ja
Kalya Nam Goli ja Bhitya nam Goli //1//

Goli Aamni Mayana lorbej lesare ja,
Kalya nam Goli ja, Bhitya nam Goli //2//

(Women are singing in a group taking names of individuals like Kalya, Bhitya, etc.)

Boys Songs - Prayer to Nature

1. *Gongolya Re Re Range, Nache Bai Kanhaiyya,*
Nache Bai Kanhaiyya //

Tuni Majya Dewa Take Raja,
Manile Majya Bai Kanhaiyya
Nache Bai Kanhaiyya //1//

Kheda'Majya Muthawa ke
Manile Raja, Bai Manile,
Nache Bai Kanhaiyya //2//

Dharati Aasman garja tinken
Raja Majya bai Kanhaiyya //3//

Boys sing this song when winds are blowing and thundering is going on. Boys/men dance in the month of *Chaitra* and *Vaisakha* standing in two circles. The first group sings, moving forward and backward and the other circle repeats it.
(Lord Kanhaiyya is dancing, the earth and sky is thundering, O, my Muthua God please listen to our request and bless with good showers of rain. O Kanhaiyya, dance and bless us.)

2. *Bebena Binato Golan Binaye*
Nache nam Re - - - //

Tone ma Dewa Kaleja Kot,
Bebena Binato Nache nam Re //1//

Khela ja Muthawa Kaleja Kot

Nache nam Re - - - //2//

Tone ma Dewa Kaleja Kot,
Nache nam Re //3//

Chande ma Surajo Kaleja Kot
Nache nam Re //4//

This is also a Gongolya song pleasing Muthua God, Sun God, etc., so that there should be good monsoon.

Description of a Beautiful Lady :

The Korku concept of an ideal beautiful lady is reflected in the following song where the girl (*Mala*) is addressed as a Gondoni, i.e., a Gond woman and hence the name is Malai-Gondoni.

Jaisa bana tinjken, Malai Gondoni do
Jaisa bana tinjken, Malai Gondoni re ///1//

Amani tingdi do, Malai Chojama do
Jaisa bana tinjken, Malai Gondoni re

Kelani Khambo nido ama tengdi mado
Jaisa bana ......

Amani bulu do, Malai Chanjani do
Jaisa bana ....

Tekla jeni poptani do, ama bulum do
Jaisa bana ....

Amani bhujani do, Malai chojani do
Jaisa bana ....

Hanini lato nido bhuja mado
Jaisa bana ....

Amani chabo nido Malai Chojani do
Tamra burujni do, ama chabuma do
Jaisa bana ....

Amani bhu nido Malai chojama do
Jaisa bana ....

Ravani chachu Keja, abha muni do
Jaisa bana ....

Charmuru petyani do, abha gala ma do
Jaisa bana ....

Amani met nido, Malai chojama do
Jaisa bana ....

Chandoma Surjo Keja, ama met nido
Jaisa bana ....

[The beautiful woman Malai Gondoni is hand pounding grains by pounding stump in the hollow pounding stone and its rhythmic sound is coming. She has put on a nice *petticoat, Challa* (ring) in finger and a nice blouse. Her face is looking like a red watermelon, her nose like a parrot, her legs look like the trunk of a banana tree and her eyes are bright like moon and sun. This woman is looking still more beautiful as she is pounding grains.]

'Tinjken' is an onomatopoeic sound of the pounding work.

Some vivid descriptions of nature are found in some songs, e.g.,

Bhiulare bhiulare badel oothe
Jer meri, jer meri pani na barse
badel bhiula.

(Slowly black clouds are collecting in the sky, and the rain is slowly drizzling.)

Chandni me chip gayo chand,
Zalak rahi chandni;
Chanda Zure oka Chandni, Suraj zure,
Oka jod, zalak rahi chandni

When a young girl is married to an old or blind or lame man she cannot enjoy life but if she is married to a young boy both are happy. This is described in a song which is rhythmic and shows good...alliteration...

Jodi do bago me, rinay jodi bago me,
Sana tota ghataen do, Kone talan tataba totaba,
Andhada tota ghataen do, Kone talan tataba totaba
Poyra tota ghataen do, Kone talan landba do mandiba.

Attraction to Forest

Pyare Jangla me Boli re
Lawara re titora,
Parbat Bole do Mor
Malani ho, me to Chala re Jangla me lal //1//

Ek roti pohe, do roti pohe
Mai to chala re Bhukha Pyasa //2//

Husband says to wife :
[O, my dear, I am going to forest where I can see *Titar* (Birds) and the peacocks on the mountains. You may give me one or two *rotis* (*Chapatis*) as my tiffin but now I am going to forest.]

Song on Need of Education

Iskul Padhe Mama
Eskul Padhe te //

Kariyale dada Ro ss Ro ss Ro
Likhyae Padhai ma kare ss re
Eskul Padhe te //1//

College Padhe mama
College Padhe te,
Kariyale dada ro
Likhaye Padhai ma Kare ss re
Iskul Padhe te //2//

B.A. Padhe mama
B.A. Padhe, te,
Kariyale dada ro

Likhaye Padhai ma kare ss re
Eskul Padhe te //3//

(O, Mama, go and study in a school. Study reading and writing. Study in College and study up to B.A. level, read and write.)

Conceptualization of a new Era of Wants

Control Ka Jamana Aaya re Babulal,
control ka Jamana Aaya re

Zakkar Ho gai Control Babulal
Control Ka Jamana Aaya re

(This era is of 'Controls' O Babulal, the '*Jamana*' (era) of controls has come to stay.)

Hansli bana risna Bagomalaya Jambado
Mundini bana risna Bagomalaya Jambado
Polka ban risna Bagomalaya Jambado

(The girl Jambomala is weeping because she does not get necklace, ring and blouse.)

This short song depicts the financial strain and its effect on fulfilling.

FOLK-TALES

Folk-tale about the Origin of Mankind

Once, when there was no mankind, all 36 crore Gods assembled under a big Banyan tree (*Bargat Peda*) and decided to create mankind. They asked the *Kaglia-masa*, i.e., a crow, to bring same earth from the sea-coast region. The crow flew but lost its feathers on the way and started walking on feet. After reaching the sea-coast the crow asked for earth from the *Katkom* (Crab) which was on the sea-coast. The crab refused but later agreed to give earth on loan, with a condition that it must be returned some day. The crow brought the earth to the Gods who prepared statues out of it and kept them for drying during night. At night fairies alighted and destroyed the statues. The Gods would again make them and fairies destroyed them. Ultimately the Gods created a dog which guarded the statues at night and saved them from fairies. Then God blew life in those statues and man was created. Thus, dog is man's friend since the day of creation.

However, the mankind could not grow and the early men were tired of that static life. The other tale describes how the human society grew in numbers maintaining social organization.

Tale about Creation of Clans (Gotras)

Korku men and women lived happily. But later they developed sex urge and could not know what to do as all considered each other as brothers and sisters. So all went to Lord Mahadeo and asked him to solve their problem. Lord Mahadeo yawned in a fierce manner and assumed a terrible form. The earth and universe shuddered. A deluge came on earth, so all Korku men and women ran away in sheer disorder and every one tried to hide behind any object they found. Thus, after the deluge was over – i.e., after years – they came out from their hidings and again went to Mahadeo, who by then had calmed down. Then they asked him about their problem. Mahadeo asked them where they had hidden. Korku replied that they had taken shelter behind trees, grass, creepers, soil and several natural objects. Mahadeo told them that their *Gotras* will be according to the tree, creeper or any other object of their hidings and that they shall marry outside their *Gotra*. Thus exogamic, totemic clans came into existence. Those who had hidden nearer to each other were also considered as brothers and hence marriages between them were also discouraged. Thus, came the clans and social order.

An old folk-tale relates to the *Nanad-Bhaujai* (Husband's sister - Brother's wife) relationship. The parents went for pilgrimage. *Nanad* asked her *Bhaujai* to give her saree for use. She refused. Hence, *Nanad* tried it in her absence which was later known to *Bhaujai*. *Bhaujai* was enraged and vowed to use saree soaked in Nanad's blood. Accordingly she killed her through her husband (i.e., got his sister killed through him) but the dead *Nanad* was converted into a flower. One youth got that flower and the girl came out of it.

Mantras also form part of the folk-lore. There is a *Mantra* supposed to ward off a tiger.

The folk-tales in Korkus are limited to the early stages of development of mankind. Even these are often narrated through the folk songs which are sung on festive occasions. Narration in story form is rare.

Heartland, in his "The Science of Fairy Tales", says, ...

The folk-tale cannot be separated from the folk-song with which, in its origin and development, it is closely connected. In India, there are, or were, until recent years, everywhere professional bards and the stories told in Indian villages are frequently the substance of the chants of these bards. More than this the line between singing and narration is so faintly drawn that the bards themselves often interpose great patches of prose between the material portions of their recitations.

There is some thinking about the astronomical objects like Sun, Moon, the seven-star configuration (*Sapta-rishi*), the Meteors, etc., and bad and good omens are associated with their position. Eclipses are considered as attacks of demons on Sun and Moon. Many interpretations based on the astronomical features are used for deciding the sowing and other agricultural operations, etc.

Among Korkus, vulgar words have status and significance on certain occasions. On '*Phool jagni*'– occasion, when the women dance– the men-folk utter vulgar words. It is not singing as such but a rhythmic utterance of words. They believe that due to such utterances the soul of the dead man gets peace and emancipation.

Tale of the Rahi Temple

Baghdoh is a small village Near it is a small lake called Sun and Moon lake which is prepared by constructing a dam over the rivers *Chandra* (Moon) and *Surya* (Sun). Outside the village there is a small temple called the Rahi Temple. The tale about this temple is narrated by old men as under :

> In a village near Baghdoh there was a youth Govind Rahi who was a shepherd. He once went to the Chandra-Surya lake and entered the palace of the Baghdoh king with other Korkus. The King had died one year back during a hunting expedition. The queen who was a widow saw Rahi and was infatuated towards him and kept him as attorney in the palace. Later, he saw a young girl on the lake and fell in love with her and wanted to marry her. The queen persuaded him not to marry her, but he did not change his mind. The queen employed Balai tribals to kill him. They caught him at night, killed him and threw the body in the Chandra-Surya lake. The girl who was to marry him also committed suicide. Thus, the Thakur queen (i.e., of Rajput origin) avenged her anger on him but later

repented and with the help of Korkus built the temple on the banks of the lake called the temple of Rahi in which Rahi's marble statue was erected. A big Kav tree spreads its shadow over the temple.

CONCLUSIONS

The foregoing pages show that the Korkus have a rich treasure of folk-lore, particularly in the form of folk-songs. Even the folk-tales are mostly in the form of songs. The collection in the foregoing pages – though not exhaustive – is adequate to represent different types of cultural genre and reflect their historical and traditional outlook to nature, society, family relationships and their total environment.

However, whatever changes have came to stay due to spread of education, better living conditions, better clothing, some farm inputs, etc., the cultural fibre has not changed. Their festivals, ceremonies, worship of Gods and Goddesses remain unaffected. Naturally the folk-lore connected with all these aspects is also still alive. Even the outlook behind these is maintained. Both the spiritual/philosophical as well as temporal characteristics are still present in their culture as reflected by their folk-songs.

Preservation versus Change

In preserving their folk-literature Korkus have allowed it to grow and get richer by adopting influences and images from the surrounding natural and social environment. Though ethno-centric, like any other tribal group, they have also adopted by introjection certain symbols, norms, styles from the predominant communities like the Yadavs/Gaulis and Thakurs who, for some part of history, were their chieftains. Later, they have also adopted many things from the Hindi and Marathi-speaking populations from the plains – from Madhya Pradesh and Vidarbha – Maharashtra, respectively. Such adoptions and adjustments in folk-literature are instances of socio-cultural change and even the dynamism or ability to grow reflect in their culture.

Even contemporary themes, ideas, images, etc., have been accepted and folk-songs based on these are sung. The styles of dress, dancing and musical instruments show these changes.

Though the collection of folk-songs, tales in the foregoing pages and the concurrent comments are sufficient to prove the above points, it will be rewarding to analyse some examples below :

Puja/Ritual Songs

Songs connected with festivals and rituals represent a very delicate cultural area wherein orthodoxy is more prominent as compared to other areas. Korkus are originally worshippers of King Ravana and on the Dussehra day while neighbouring cultural groups on the plains are praising Rama and burning the effigies of Ravana, the Korkus worship Ravana, Meghnad and Kumbhakarna. However, on other occasions they too worship Ram, Laxman, Krishna and Hanumana. Songs praising Ravana as well as Rama, Hanumana and Kanhaiyya (Krishna) evidently prove this cultural adjustment. The worship of Mahadeva and Parvati – like other tribals is not unnatural, but the prayer of Lord Ganesh and the dance-drama (Khamm) based on the worship of *Sudarshan Chakra* indicate religious acculturation. One can say that a Golden mean of diverging faiths has been struck by them and consequently a cross-fertilization of culture-enriching and culture broadening. The historical influence of the Rajputs (Yadav, Thakur and others) is obvious, followed by that of neighbours from the plains.

The Philosophical and Materialistic Songs

While the philosophical songs preach the futility of earthly pleasures and attachment in a very effective manner, other songs advocate the use and greatness of *Sona-rupa* (Gold, Silver) and other earthly matters.

The Divine and the Profane Songs

While there are songs for worshipping deities and involving spiritual aspects, there are songs which plunge into vulgarity and sex. Thus, both the aspects of human life find place in Korku folk-songs. One can easily make out by reading the songs that some divinity and some profanity are adopted from outside.

The Brother-Sister Affection Songs

The *Jeroti* songs depicting the affection of sister towards her brother represent a finer aspect of their culture. Even in the Rajput culture the brother-sister relationship is given a significant place in folk-lore. Though similar sentiments must be existing among Korkus, some consolidation of those sentiments under Rajput rulership cannot be ruled out. Contemporary influences are seen even in other type of songs.

The Love Songs

Those depicting love between boy and girl, husband and wife, etc., are replete with various similies and metaphors – many based on items exotic to their tribal culture. Maybe, some time in distant historical past they were introduced to these things but now they have adopted these ideas as a part of their culture. Idea of a golden plate (*Sone Ke Thali*) or a golden door (*Sone Ka Darwaja*) and a goldsmith from Bombay, etc., are signs of a high level of acculturation.

The fear and harassment caused to the newly married bride by the in-laws, her emotional attachment to her parents and the moments of finer or delicate love with her lover/husband are brought out in many songs in a nice manner.

The songs for children – particularly for lulling them – are very simple but demonstrate the imagination of composer. The use of words is also suitable for the tuning and singing of songs in a lulling style.

Songs on Nature

Trees, sky, sun, moon, stars, moon-lit nights, rivers, wells, birds, thundering clouds and rains – all form the subject-matter of songs describing nature or using metaphors from nature, e.g.,

> *"Chandni Rato Kokodo,*
> *Chandni Rat Kuldailala"* //

Peacocks, cuckoo, rabbits, bears and trees of *jamun, neem,* bamboo, etc., all are utilized as illustrations for expressing sentiments. Personification – though remote – is attempted.

Story of creation of earth appears to be somewhat scientific. The black sky (absence of moon), gaseous earth, etc., are factors nearer to some theories of creation. Their astronomical knowledge also sounds to be pseudo scientific. This knowledge is inherited since generations and it is difficult to decide whether it was adopted from outside or their own forefathers thought and understood phenomena.

Reflections of Modern Era

Modern objects, events, situations are also reflected in some songs. There is reference to control era (control *Ka Zamana*) and also to the importance of education. This shows that they know, reflect and can put into words the developments which affect them or engross their minds.

Folk-Tales

The folk-tales are in the form of songs and are presented in song form only. On certain occasions the old-men go on reciting tale-songs for hours together, i.e., for five to six hours or throughout the night. At times this '*Katha*' is purpose-oriented – to propitiate some God. It was reported that when there is drought '*Katha*' (stories) continued and by the time '*Katha-Kathan*' (story-telling) is over rains arrive. History of mankind, or of their Korku tribe or of particular clan, stories about God, nature, etc., form the subject-matter. But it is difficult to get pure 'tales' as against 'songs'. It is important to remember that verses are easy to memorise than prose. (Our great epics are also in verse form.) These tales serve educative purpose because knowledge is passed to new generation through them.

It is obvious that the Korku folk-literature, traditionally passed on from generation to generation, is still in vogue and represents the historical cultural perspective of their tribe. Through ages they have grown richer due to additions from their own tribesmen and also due to influence of surrounding cultures. The socio-cultural changes have also been in the nature of adjustments with the changing social environment. Even contemporary ideas due to modernization have been incorporated though on a modest scale. Thus, the tribal genre is not dying out but adjusting and growing.

Songs are sung as a matter and part of their daily routine life, and is community entertainment. Even while working they sing songs, though it is a must on occasions.

The collection of Korku folk-lore and the analyses show that :

(i) The Korku tribals in the Melghat area are having a rich store of folk-lore inherited, among which the folk-songs are predominant and the folk-tales are also narrated in the form of songs. These are sung on various occasions and while dancing.

(ii) The folk-literature of Korkus (not strictly folk-tales but songs) contains information about their socio-cultural history, and also about the contemporaneous changes in their socio-cultural life.

(iii) By interpreting the contents of these pieces or oral literature, acquaintance with their socio-cultural characteristics is possible.

(iv) Influence of the surrounding cultures and an alertness to changing environment – resulting in adjustment – leading to preservation as well as growth is seen in their folk-literature. The genre of Korkus is quite alive and responsive to changing situations.

(v) Rich treasure of folk-literature is available and must be augmented before it passes out of hands.

NINE

DEVELOPMENT OF THE KORKU TRIBALS

Since long, Korkus are cattle-keepers and farmers. Shifting cultivation has almost stopped. Improved agricultural practices are being adopted, though slowly. Working as labourers in forests and on farms is common. They are introduced and attached to money and, in many villages, their eagerness to earn money was explicit.

In the Dharni and Chikhaldara Tribal Development (T.D.) Blocks, development activities have yielded good results. The I.T.D.P. at Dharni and the tribal sub-plan schemes have helped the tribals in improving their living. Electrification work has covered 50-75 per cent villages in the area. The Tribal Area Research Project of the Punjabrao Krishi Vidyapeeth (Agricultural University), Akola, has its field units at Dharni and Chickhaldara under Senior Scientists. They have done good work in the sphere of agricultural extension, and home science and also helped research in the area.

The changes in the physical culture like dress, style of housing and occupation are not significant considering the schemes for their development. Style of housing is also traditional though Manglore Tiles appear on a few roofs. Agriculture, though not primitive, is not modernized even. Though electrification has been done, except street lights (and a few domestic connections in well-to-do houses) individual families could not get the benefits of electricity. Communication has improved to some extent, though there are still villages not well connected by roads and that too all-weather roads. One has to climb down hills to reach the village, facing the perils of wild animals.

Even then one has to admit that the spread of education, communication with other progressive areas and the work done by development agencies have definitely helped in accelerating the process of acculturation and facilitated adoption of many new practices. Shifting cultivation has almost stopped and improved agricultural practices are adopted by many of them.

The Kalyan Ashram, a voluntary organization, has started medical social work under a team of doctors at and around Chikhaldara and is getting good response from the Korku tribals. Previously only the Christian Mission was doing this type of work.

The Tribal Sub-Plan Schemes

The Project Officer, I.T.D.P., Dharni, informed that the specific schemes implemented under the Nucleus budget included the following during the year 1986-87 :

Preparatory facilities and guidance for military recruitment
Training facility for stenography
Vocational guidance
Training in tailoring
Promotion of arts and skills
Special coaching for S.S.C. students
Trades for tribal youths
Supply of pipe, etc., for irrigation
Supply of cows
Transport subsidy for bringing buffaloes
Repairs to huts (tiles, etc.) (on 75 per cent subsidy)
Electrification (on 75 per cent subsidy)
Supply of uniforms to school children and to *Anganwadi* Children
Supply of sports material and *Shamiana* and loudspeaker, etc.

The Tiger Project

The Melghat Tiger Reserve Project of the Government of Maharashtra has affected the life of the Korku population. It is located in the Chikhaldara area and covers the core area of 308.24 sq. km *plus* a buffer area of 1288.99 sq. km, the total area being 1598.23 sq. km.

In the sanctum sanctorum, no fellings, grazing or movements of men are permitted. Anti-poaching and protection operations are strengthened and habitat development is manipulated to suit the wildlife. In the core area there are no villages but in the buffer area there are 54 villages, the human population amounting to 16,202 and cattle population 16,743. Entry of humans or cattle in the core area is strictly prohibited and 17 barricades with 24 hours strict vigilance are erected.

This is supported with shot-gun wielding staff (for anti-social elements), wireless communication, etc.

Payment of compensation is made to owners of cattle whenever cattle in the 'buffer' area is killed by tigers/leopard as per the conditions of the government.

However, all forest activities, including labour work, picking of minor forest produce, farming in the buffer area, communication through the area, etc., are affected to the disadvantage of the local tribal population. There is also a proposal to shift six villages which are situated very close to the boundary of the core area on South-Eastern side, viz., Bairat, Pastalai, Shahanpur, Aladah, Churni and Lawada, where the villagers have milch cattle. They will get all possible facilities and full infrastructure elsewhere. However, this has not yet been finalized due to political pressure.

Considering the vast expanse of the Korku population in the Melghat area the problem of the Tiger Reserve Project is localized and does not have extremely wide impact on the life of the Korku population in general. Those living in the vicinity of the core area or in the buffer area are affected, but considering the compensation (Rs. 60,000 paid during 1984-85 for loss of cattle) and the fact that there are no villages in the 'core' area, the negative impact – if any – is not alarming. We visited the village Pastalai and found the tribal population quite happy and had no complaints to offer. However, it was reported that the *Nistar* rights in the area have been affected. Easy and short-route communication is disturbed and many petty farmers and farm labourers have become jobless due to strict restrictions imposed in the area. Much hue and cry raised seems to be more a part of politics and rumour-mongering than a real one.

On the contrary, the whole area under the project – including the 'buffer' and the outskirts – is being developed with road improvement and special veterinary care to prevent the outbreak of foot and mouth disease in domestic cattle from the adjoining villages.

The project is relevant only in the Chikhaldara block and not in the Dharni area.

APPENDICES

APPENDIX I

SOME KORKU WORDS

Relations

Jimu - Name
Inj - I
Dai - Brother
Bai - Sister
Ai/Mai - Mother
Aaba - Father
Japai - Wife
Shana-Aaba - Grandfather
Shani-mai - Grandmother
Oo (as in ooze) - Brother's wife
Kaka - Uncle
Kaki - Uncle's wife
Jawai - Son-in-law,
Sasra - Father-in-law,
Samdi - The in-laws
Mama - Maternal uncle
Mami - Maternal Uncle's wife
Sani - Child
Tare - Girl
Por - Boy
Kon - Son
Konje - Daughter

Utensils, etc.

German - Aluminium
Pitala - Brass
Steela - Steel (Stainless)
Gilla - Glass for water
Churu - A round tumbler ('*Lota*' in Hindi)
Thala - Metal plate
Bhogona - A big metal plate
Gundo - *Gaghar* (a round utensil for water storage made of brass)
Balti - Bucket
Seedu - Beer
Mu-Seedu - Liquor of *Mahua* tree

Nature

Da - Water
Kasa - Soil

Seenj - Tree
Kende - Black
Rata - Red
Kheeti - Farm/ agriculture
Koroku - Men
Zanay - Woman
Ambe-seenj - Mango tree
Sipna seenj - Teak tree
Limbu seenj - Lemon tree
Santra seenj - Orange tree
Kande - Onion
Lusun - Garlic
Mircha - Chili
Sasan - Turmeric
Dhega - Stone

Animals

Bakra - He goat
Sheli - She goat
Doba - Bullock
Gauku - Cow
Bitakel - Buffalo
Simku - Hen
Komba - Cock
Mara - Peacock
Kwali - Rabbit
Kolya - Jackal
Dhak - Deer
Jilu - Mutton/meat

Numerals

Moya - One
Bariya - Two
Afya - Three
Oofoon/ufoon - Four
Monoya - Five
Turuya - Six
Eya - Seven
Itar - Eight
Aareya - Nine
Gel - Ten
Gyara - Eleven
Visa - Twenty
Chaliso - Forty
Satho - Sixty
Mona isa or *Miyasadi* - Hundred
Miya Rupya - One rupee
Rupya - Rupee
Dama - Paise

Korku Limbs

Ti - Hand
Mil - Nose
Chabu - Mouth
Lutur - Ear
Kapar - Head
Laj - Belly
Nanga - Foot
Med, Met - Eye
Tiring - Tooth
Hup - Hair
Lang - Tongue
Bhauri - Back

Metals

Sunna - Gold
Loh, Lokhando - Iron
Chandi - Silver

General

Bhagya - Slave
Gadri - Shepherd
Bhagwan - Devil

Tende gomaj - Moon
Singel, tsingel - Fire
Ura - House
Gai - Cow
Minu - Cat
Badako - Duck
Unto - Camel
Sene, ba - Go
Subange - Sit
Ura, Kisan - Cultivator
Gomoej, gomoi, gomej - God
Gomoi, gomoej - Sun
Ipil - Star
Da - Water
Gurgi - Horse
Sita, tisita - Dog
Komba - Cock
Gadri - Ass
Titit - Bird
Jome, Jijume - Eat
Heje - Come
Tengine - Stand
Ile - Give
Len - Up
Itan - Down
Sutukin - Before
Ye - Who
Chojika - Why
Metin - But
He, aa, Ji, Woi - Yes
Hay hay - Alas
Aba - Of a father
Abuten abate - From a father
Abako - Fathers
Abakoa - Of fathers
Abakoten - From fathers
Konjea - Of a daughter
Konjelen - From a daughter
Konjeko - Daughters
Konjeken - To daughters
Awal koro - A good man
Awal koroken - To good men
Awal koroking - Two good men
Awal korokoa - Of good man
Awal Kerote - From good men
Baka pohar - A bad boy
Baka tare - A bad girl
Dusaro-ten
Awal - Better
Uncha - High
Uncha - Highest
Japai Gurgi - A mare
Japai Gurgiko - Mares
Gai - A Cow
Gaiko - Cows
Kwage - Beat
Goie - Die
Saurube - Run
Meran - Near
Lanka, dills, Sangin - Far
Tawen - Behind
Choch - What
Eta, Do - And
Dare - It
Bang, He-bang, Baki - No
Aba - A father
Aba-ken aba-ke - To a father
Baria aba, Abuking - Two fathers
Abakoken - To father
Konje - A daughter

Konjeken	- To a daughter	*Sitako*	- Dogs
Konjeking	- Two daughters	*Bokra*	- A he-goat
Konjekoa	- Of daughters	*Bokroko*	- Goats
Konjekote	- From daughters	*Japai Chitali*	- Female deer
Awal korva	- Of good man	*Ing tijka*	- I am
Awal Korote	- From good man	*Di tikya*	- He is
Awal Koroku	- Good men	*Ape tijako*	- You are
Awal Koroken	- To good men		
Awal japay	- A good woman		
Awal Japayko	- Good Women		
Awal	- Good		
Saboten Awal	- Best		
Uncha	- Higher		
Gurgi	- A horse		
Gurgko	- Horses		
Doba	- A bull		
Dobako	- Bulls		
Sita	- A dog		
Japai Sita	- A bitch		
Japai-sitako	- Bitches		
Siri	- She-goat		
Darkar-Chitali	- Amale deer		
Chitali	- Deer		
Am tikya	- You are		
Abung takako	- We are		

Pieces of Conversation in Korku :

Ama jeemu chuj?	-What is your name?
Iya jeemu Shankar	- My name is Shankar
Ama aba jeemu chuj?	- What is your father's name?
Iya aba jeemu Goma	- My father's name is Goma
Ama jato chuj?	- What is your Surname?
Iya jato Chilati	- My Surname is Chilati

Amen choto Daiku?	- How many brothers have you?
Iyan Barkom daiku taka	- I have two brothers
Amen choto baiku taka?	- How many sisters have you?
Ingeke afiya baiku taka	- I have three sisters
Amen japai taka ki ban?	- Do you have a wife?
Iyan Japai taka	- I have a wife
Ama aba chuj kamay wa?	- What is your father's job?
Iya aba Khiti Kamay wa	- My father works on farm
Ama dai chuj kamay?	- What is your brother's job?
Iya dai Khiti kamay wa	- My brothers work on farm
Ama meran Khiti taka ki ban?	- Do you have a farm?
Iya meran Khiti taka	- I have farms
Ama ata noke ki chuj?	- Did you take meals?
Ing ata jokey	- Yes, I had meals
Ama uran chuja Sokla ondar/ke?	- Which (or what) bread do you eat?
Iya uran jondra Sokla taka	- I have juar bread at my place
Am tenj tuman senewa?	- Where do you go today?
Inj tenj ati senewa	- Today I go to bazaar
Am Amravatin chola senewa?	- When will you go to Amravati?
Ama Jumu Choch?	- What is your name?
Ing gurgi-ken Chota orso-ko?	- How old is this horse?
In-en-te Kasmiran lank an Choch?	- How far is it from here to Kashmir?
Ama aba uran chota Konku?	- How many sons are there in your father's house?

Ing Kha-lanka eje	- I have walked a long way today
Iya kaka konten konja salane bi-yao-kane	- The son of my uncle is married to his sister
Phulum ghudgi fin uran	- In the house is the saddle of the white horse
Ghudgi pataliyem fin andaya	- Put the saddle upon his back
Ing dija kon-te-kan khut kwolla-te Kwa-Khane	- I have beaten his son with many stripes
Ahu koho tikadi gayku chara -anda-ken	- He is grazing cattle on the top of the hill
Dija dada dija bai-te ucha	- His brother is taller than his sister
Aya aba sani uran thar-ba	- My father lives in that house
De rupiya dije ikki	- Give this rupee to him
Di kui-ten da kolage	- Draw water from the well

BOTANICAL TERMS FOR THE TREES/PLANTS

Bhilawa	- *Semecarpus anacardium*
Barbati	- *Vigna catjang*
Ber	- *Zizyphus jujuba*
Barai (Sugarcane)	- *Saccharum officinarum*
Bete/Sewan	- *Gmelina arborea*
Chironji	- *Buchanania latifolia*
Chilati	- *Caesalpinia sepiaria*
Dhan/Rice	- *Oryza sativa*
Dhawda	- *Anogeissus latifolia*
Gurgi	- *Coix lachryma*
Jamun/Jambu	- *Eugenia jambolana*
Kullu	- *Sterculia urens*
Kodo	- *Paspalum scrobiculatum*
Kutki	- *Panicum psilopodium*
Mahul	- *Bauhinia vahlii*
Mandgi	- *Elusine coreana*
Mahua	- *Bassia latifolia*
Mango	- *Mangifera indica*
Neem	- *Azadirachte indica*
Rala (*Kangni*)	- *Setaria italica*
Sag (Teak)	- *Tectona grandis*
Sal	- *Shorea Robusta*
Salai	- *Boswellia serrata*
Tendu	- *Diospyros melanoxylon*
Toor	- *Cajunus cajan*

BIBLIOGRAPHY

Anonymous, (1911). *Census of India.*

Basu, Arbinda, (1970). Anthropology of the Korku Melghat Forest. *Man In India*, 50(2).

Bhagwat Durga, *Loksahtyachi Roopresha.*

Bhagwat Durga, *Dharma Aani Loksahitya.*

Crooke, W., *The Popular Religion and Folk-lore of Northern India*, I & II.

Fitzgerald, S.V. and Nelson, A.E., (1911). *Central Provinces District Gazetteers*, Amravati District, A, Descriptive.

Government of India, (1929). *Melghat Manual* (Government Publication for office use).

Grierson, G.A., *Linguistic Survey of India*, IV (Munda & Dravidian Languages).

Karve, Iravati, *Marathi Lokanchi Sanskriti* (Marathi).

Kale, Yadav Madhav, *Nagpurkar Bhoslyancha Itihas* (Marathi).

Kulkarni, K.P., *Marathi Bhasha - Udgam ani Vikas* (Marathi).

Mandavkar, Bhau, *Aadim.*

Mande, Prabhakar, *Loksahityache Swarup.*

Mande, Prabhakar, *Loksahityache Antapravah.*

Maharashtra Loksahitya Samiti, *Maharashtra Loksahitya Mala Pushpa Chauthe.*

Nadgonde, Gurunath, *Bhartiya Adivasi.*

Padmanabha, P., *General Population and Population of Scheduled Castes and Scheduled Tribes.*

Russel, R.V. & Hiralal, *Tribes and Castes of the Central Provinces of India*, III.

PHOTOGRAPHS

PHOTO 1: Shrine of Muthua — the local God of Korku villages

PHOTO 2: Korku men at Pastalai

PHOTO 3: Shri Arjun Jade Patel *alias* Arjun Guruji of Tingrya (near Dharni)

PHOTO 4: Smt. Yashodabai Mavaskar *alias* Nanibai from Dharni — A Korku social worker honoured with the Adivasi — Sevak Award by Govt. of Maharashtra in 1988

PHOTO 5: At Khaparkheda (near Dharni), Korku girls (in Sarees — Gujarathi style) singing at Bhayai

PHOTO 6: Shri Arjun Jade Patel *alias* Arjun (Guruji) (wearing turban) with the author at Tingrya (near Dharni)

PHOTO 7: Korku women at Tetu

PHOTO 8: *Patelan* at *Kharya* — see profuse tatooing on her forehands

PHOTO 9: Korku men with the Patel of the village

PHOTO 10: A Korku woman in Paratwada Market—Mark the Traditional style 9-yard saree

INDEX